"Christianity's Jewish Roots: A Study of Judaism for Christians explores the amazing journey into the origins of the Christian faith. Susan created a must-read in understanding Christianity's deep connection to Jewish history. Organized and easy to follow, the book is ideal for Sunday School classes, Bible studies, or individuals interested in their heritage."

–Diane Greenwood Muir, Author
Bellingwood series
Mage's Odyssey series

"Susan Renni Anderson has done a stellar job. Christianity's Jewish Roots: A Study of Judaism for Christians takes you on a fascinating journey into every Christian's ancestry. Susan has created a must-read in understanding Christianity's deep connection to Jewish History. This is an easy read, easy to follow study. Christianity's Jewish Roots is ideal for small groups, church retreats, or individuals interested in their heritage."

–Rev. Scott Simpson Associate Pastor for Congregational Care First Presbyterian Church, San Antonio, TX

CONTENTS

Christianity's Jewish Roots

A Study of Judaism for Christians

Christianity's Jewish Roots

A Study of Judaism for Christians

Susan Renni Anderson

Published by Mountain Side Publishing

ISBN (paperback): 979-8-9870904-0-4
ISBN (ebook): 979-8-9870904-1-1

Printed in the United States of America

To Hamilton Mill United Methodist Church and to Senior Associate Pastor Jason Mincey. Without your encouragement and support this book would never have happened. You peeled away the layers and opened the way for the Holy Spirit to guide me. Thank you just isn't enough.

INTRODUCTION

"Listen to me, you pursuers of justice, you who see ADONAI: consider the rock from which you were cut, the quarry from which you were dug—consider Avraham your father and Sarah who gave birth to you; in that I called him when he was only one person, then blessed him and made him many."

ISAIAH 51:1-2 (*COMPLETE JEWISH BIBLE*)

WHY DO CHRISTIANS NEED TO LEARN ABOUT JUDAISM?

There are five important reasons:

1. **Christians need to learn about Judaism to understand their own heritage.** Christianity arose from Judaism. The entire Bible and all of its authors were Jewish. Jesus was a Jewish teacher, and his Apostles were Jewish. Jesus' audience was Jewish. Jesus was born and raised as a Torah-observant Jew. He was considered a rabbi and taught the people like a rabbi. Therefore, Christianity is inextricably bound up and related to Judaism. So, we will seek to answer the questions:

   ✡   What is Judaism?
   ✡   What are the traditional Jewish beliefs?
   ✡   What are the traditional Jewish practices?

2. **Christians need to learn about Judaism to better understand the New Testament.** Because the New Testament is a collection of Jewish writings, it naturally contains Jewish concepts, terms, and philosophies. Most Christians do not fully grasp the significance of these Jewish ideas. Chief among these is "the law." Jesus Himself clearly affirmed the Torah when He said: *"Do not think that I have come to abolish the Law but to fulfill them. For truly I tell you, until heaven and earth disappear, not the smallest letter, not the least stroke of a pen, will by any means disappear from the Law until everything is accomplished (Matthew 5:17-18.)*

3. **Christians need to recognize that Jesus came to fulfill what God had spoken and was written in the five books of Moses and the prophets.** Many Christians believe that the law is the Ten Commandments. While the law certainly includes the Ten Commandments, there is more to the law—much more. We will therefore ask:

    ✡   What is the law?
    ✡   Who is bound by the law?
    ✡   Who wrote the law?
    ✡   What was Jesus' view of the law?

4. **Christians need to learn about Judaism to obtain a deeper understanding of Jesus.** Every Christian wants to be able to envision Jesus the man: who he was and what he did, especially in everyday life. Jesus of Nazareth was a Jew and a pious one at that. As a Galilean, he most likely had rich black hair, dark skin, brown eyes, and a full untrimmed beard. And because he lived a life unique to the descendants of Abraham, Isaac, and Jacob—when he was eight days old, he was circumcised. As

he grew older, he studied Judaism's sacred texts with the rabbis. And like any Jew, he attended synagogue prayer services and celebrated all the Jewish holidays. So, again, we have questions to answer:

- ✡ Why is circumcision so important in Judaism?
- ✡ What are Judaism's sacred texts?
- ✡ Why do Jews devote considerable time to the study of these texts?
- ✡ What is a rabbi?
- ✡ What is a synagogue?
- ✡ What is the significance of the major Jewish holidays?

5. **Christians need to learn about Judaism to participate in dialogue with their Jewish brothers and sisters.** Today, Jews and Christians enjoy a relationship of respect and friendship. But, dialogue without foundation is difficult at best. Christians would want to know:

- ✡ Who is considered a Jew?
- ✡ Do all Jews share the same beliefs?
- ✡ Do Jews believe in the coming of the Messiah?
- ✡ Why don't Jews believe that Jesus was the Messiah

Christians and Jews have the Same God and Abraham is their Common Forefather. Abraham was a Semite, a descendant of Noah's son Shem. The patriarch Abraham was the first person in the Bible to be called a Hebrew (Genesis 14:13), and both the Jewish people and Christians worldwide are the descendants of Abraham. *"And if you belong to Christ, then you are Abraham's offspring, heirs according to the promise." (Galatians 3:29)* Today there are roughly 15 million Jewish people worldwide, whose very existence is one of the most remarkable facts of history. These people are the Jews: by birth, marriage, or adoption in faith, they are all members of a single family—a family that traces its genealogy back nearly four thousand years to a Middle Eastern nomad named Abraham.

There are 5 million Jews in Israel and 6.5 million in the United States. Of the latter, 1.6 million are in New York State, and the vast majority of those are in New York City. You can see what a tiny religious group this is: six-tenths of 1 percent of the number of Christians (2.3 billion) and 1 percent of the number of Muslims (1.6 billion). But this has always been the case, even before the Holocaust. The Jewish population in the world has always been small in comparison to their overwhelming significance as a religious people. Overwhelming because their religion not only "invented" monotheism—at least after the prehistoric rise of polytheism—but it became the mother of both Christianity and Islam, the largest religions in the world.

In the United States, as in Israel and other countries, Jews are divided into two groups—religious Jews and secular Jews. The former believes in God and perpetuate the Jewish tradition in a variety of ways. The latter have either rejected the idea of God entirely or else, while still believing in God, do not believe that the Jewish tradition is the best or only way to God. Yet they take pride in the accomplishments of the Jewish people, including their spiritual creativity.

The survival of this family as a self-conscious entity through forty centuries would be enough to make the Jews a unique people. No other human family approaches it in size or antiquity. But the descendants of Abraham have survived much more than time. They have endured the most ruthless and long-continued persecution ever visited upon any people. They have clung to their family identity no matter how high the price—and that price has ranged from living in ghettoes to dying in gas chambers.

The mystery does not end there. For the Jews have not merely kept alive. They have placed an indelible mark on human civilization, and particularly on the moral and religious life of mankind. Out of this people came two of the world's great theistic religions—Judaism and Christianity. Our purpose is to examine these two "Jewish" faiths to see what they have in common and where they differ.

The description of Christianity as a Jewish faith may shock some Christians—and probably some Jews as well. Both Jews and Christians are inclined to forget how closely they are intertwined by common beliefs and a common history. But the relationship remains an intimate one, however little it may be acknowledged on either side. It is not simply a matter of Jesus being a Jew. *All* the people who wrote *All* the Bible and *All* the people who founded the Christian Church were Jews (with the possible exception of Luke, who was likely a Hellenized Jew.) And they had no intention of starting a "new" religion. For them, Christianity was a fulfillment rather than a repudiation of Judaism. The Jewish religious heritage and its essential doctrines would be quite meaningless apart from that context. The implication of these facts—which are clearly set forth in the New Testament—is that no one can become a Christian without also becoming in some sense a Jew. That is what the late Pope Pius XII meant when he said, "Spiritually, we are Semites."

Note: Unless otherwise noted, scripture is from the New Revised Standard Version

Christianity as a religion was an offshoot of Judaism. It has been said that Judaism does not need Christianity to explain its existence, but Christianity needs Judaism both to explain its existence and what it believes. Hence, Christianity has also been termed historically as the Judeo-Christian faith. In the early years of the Christian faith, Jesus' followers were regarded as just another sect of Judaism (Acts 28:22) known as the sect of the Nazarenes. The early disciples and the 12 Apostles were all Jewish. Apostle Paul even took a Nazarite vow (Numbers 6:1-21) to prove to his critics that he was a Torah-observant Jew (Acts 21:17-26). Not to be confused with the Nazarenes, a Nazarites was an Israelite consecrated to the service of God, under vows to abstain from alcohol, let the hair grow, and avoid defilement by contact with corpses.

The term 'Christians' surfaced only in AD 42 when the disciples were first called that in Antioch (Acts 11:26). Initially, the term was used flippantly and by some derogatorily. The term gradually was adopted to differentiate believing Jews from unbelieving Jews and over time, it became a separate identity altogether. ***"Do not boast over the branches. If you do boast, remember that it is not you that support the root (Israel's forefathers), but the root that supports you (Church)."*** (Romans 11:18)

Note: Unless otherwise noted, scripture is from the New Revised Standard Version

JEWISH HISTORY

Israel is the very embodiment of Jewish continuity: It is the only nation on earth that inhabits the same land, bears the same name, speaks the same language, and worships the same God that it did 3,000 years ago. You dig the soil and you find pottery from Davidic times, coins from Bar Kokhba, and 2,000-year-old scrolls written in a script remarkably like the one that today advertises ice cream at the corner candy store.

GOD'S COVENANTS WITH HIS PEOPLE

Covenants are an important feature of the Bible's teaching. Seven specific covenants are revealed in Scripture. These seven covenants fall into three categories—conditional, unconditional, and general. Conditional covenants are based on certain obligations and prerequisites; if the requirements are not fulfilled, the covenant is broken. Unconditional covenants are made with no strings attached and will be kept regardless of one party's fidelity or infidelity.

General covenants are not specific to one people group and can involve a wide range of people.

The conditional covenant mentioned in Scripture is the Mosaic Covenant; the blessings it extends are contingent upon Israel's adherence to the Law. The unconditional covenants mentioned in the Bible are the Abrahamic and Davidic Covenants; God promises to fulfill these regardless of other factors. The general covenants mentioned are the Adamic, Noahic, and New Covenants, which are global in scope. Each of these covenants is listed below in biblical order with a brief description:

1. **Edenic Covenant**—Man is charged with responsibility for propagating the race, subduing the earth, exercising dominion over the animals, caring for the garden in Eden, and refraining from eating of the tree of the knowledge of good and evil.

   "God blessed them, and God said to them, 'Be fruitful and multiply, and fill the earth and subdue it; and have dominion over the fish of the sea and over the birds of the air and over every living thing that moves upon the earth.' And God said, 'Behold, I have given you every plant yielding seed which is upon the face of all the earth, and every tree with seed in its fruit; you shall have them for food. And to every beast of the earth, and to every bird of the air, and to everything that creeps on the earth, everything that has the breath of life, I have given every green plant for food.' And it was so."(Genesis 1:28-30)

2. **Adamic Covenant**—See Genesis 3. Consequences of man's fall necessitated a changed relationship between man and God including the following elements: A curse on the serpent; the first promise a Messiah would come in the line of Seth, Noah. Shem, Abraham, Isaac, Jacob, Judah and David; a changed

state of woman including bondage and subservience to man's headship, and suffering and pain in motherhood. Loss of the garden in Eden as a dwelling place and light occupation changed to a heavy burden of work because of a cursed earth; inevitable sorrow and disappointment in life; and a shortened life span and tragedy of death.

3. **Noahic Covenant**—This general covenant was made between God and Noah following the departure of Noah, his family, and the animals from the ark. Found in Genesis 9:11, *"I establish my covenant with you, that never again shall all flesh be cut off by the waters of a flood, and never again shall there be a flood to destroy the earth."* This covenant included a sign of God's faithfulness to keep it—the rainbow.

4. **Abrahamic Covenant**—This unconditional covenant, first made to Abraham in Genesis 12:1-3, promised God's blessing upon Abraham, to make his name great and to make his progeny into a great nation. The covenant also promised blessings to those who blessed Abraham and cursing to those who cursed him. Further, God vowed to bless the entire world through Abraham's seed. Circumcision was the sign that Abraham believed the covenant (Romans 4:11). The fulfillment of this covenant is seen in the history of Abraham's descendants and in the creation of the nation of Israel. The worldwide blessing came through Jesus Christ, who was of Abraham's family line.

5. **Mosaic Covenant**—This conditional covenant, found in Deuteronomy 11 and elsewhere, promised the Israelites a blessing for obedience and a curse for disobedience. Much of the Old Testament chronicles the fulfillment of this cycle of

judgment for sin and later blessing when God's people repented and returned to God.

6. **Davidic Covenant**—This unconditional covenant, found in 2 Samuel 7:8-16, promised to bless David's family line and assured an everlasting kingdom. Jesus is from the family line of David (Luke 1:32-33) and, as the Son of David (Mark 10:47), is the fulfillment of this covenant.

7. **New Covenant**—An everlasting unconditional covenant, found in Jeremiah 31:31-34, promised that God would forgive sin and have a close, unbroken relationship with His people. The promise was first made to Israel and then extended to everyone who comes to Jesus Christ in faith (Matthew 26:28; Hebrews 9:15).

A TIMELINE OF BIBLICAL HISTORY
~Major Events From Creation to the Completion of the New Testament~

c. = circa/about

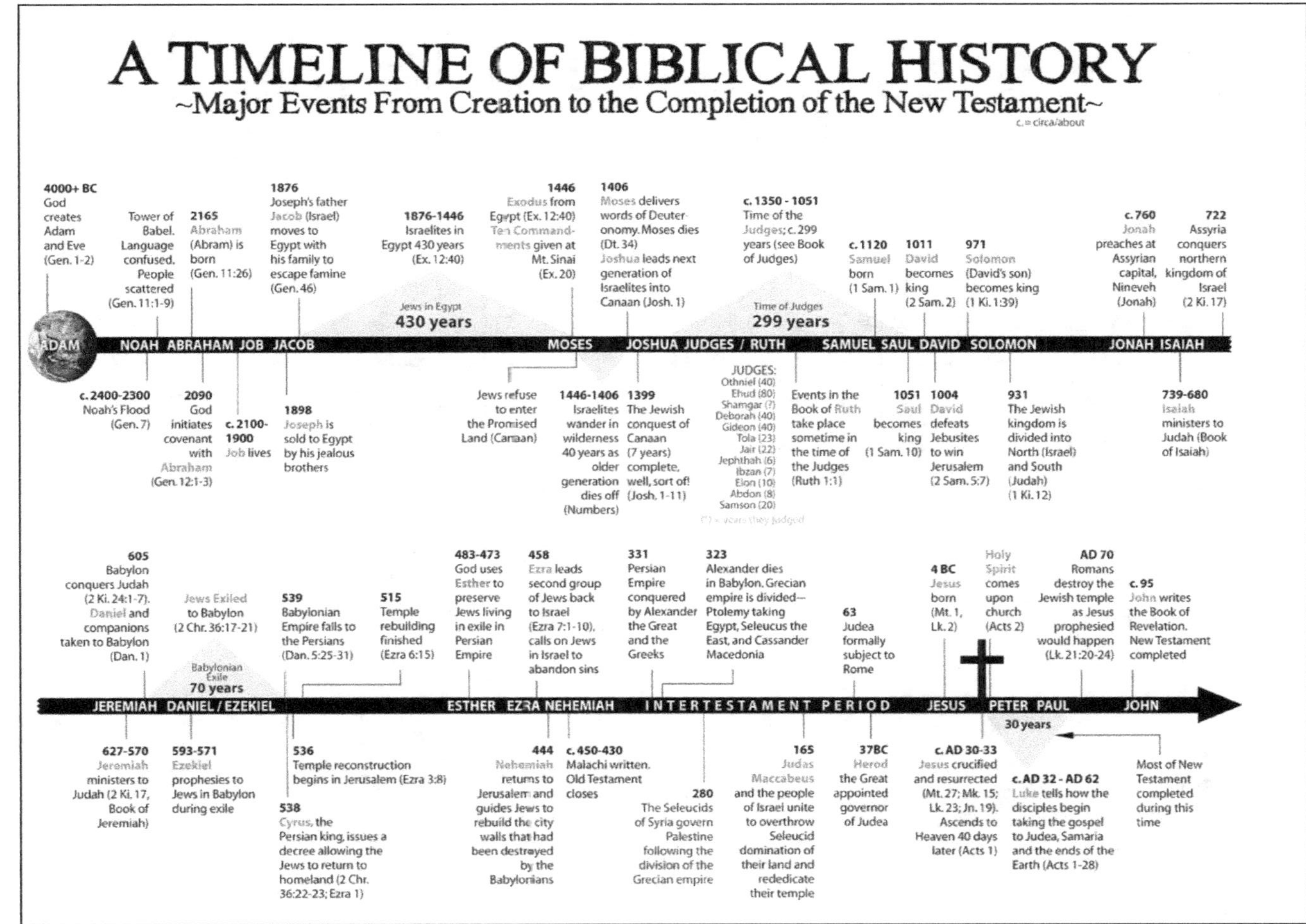

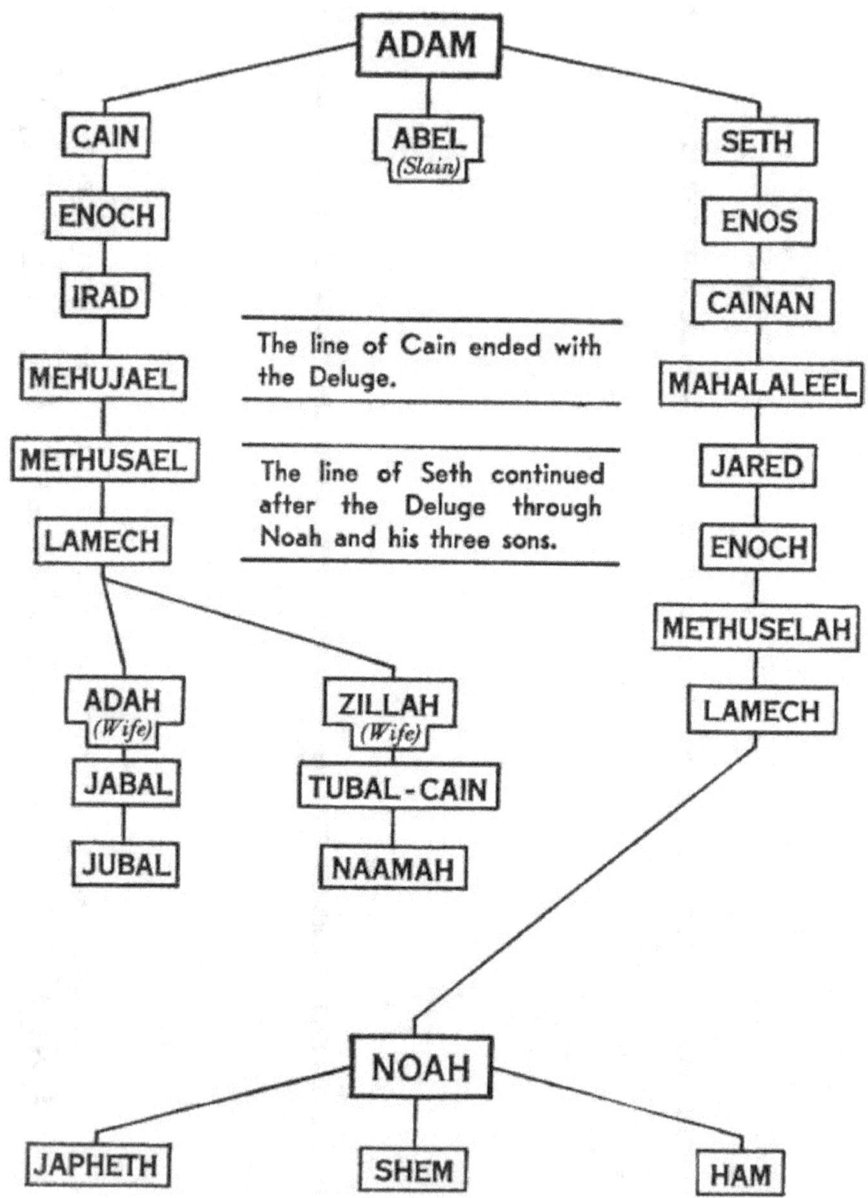
ADAM
CAIN
ABEL
(Slain)
SETH
ENOCH
ENOS
IRAD
CAINAN
The line of Cain ended with the Deluge.
MEHUJAEL
MAHALALEEL
METHUSAEL
The line of Seth continued after the Deluge through Noah and his three sons.
JARED
LAMECH
ENOCH
METHUSELAH
ADAH
(Wife)
ZILLAH
(Wife)
LAMECH
JABAL
TUBAL-CAIN
JUBAL
NAAMAH
NOAH
JAPHETH
SHEM
HAM

GENEALOGY OF JESUS APOLOGETICS PRESS

MATTHEW

LUKE

MATTHEW	LUKE
Abraham	Abraham
Isaac	Isaac
Jacob	Jacob
Judah	Judah
Perez	Perez
Hezron	Hezron
Ram	Ram
Amminadab	Amminadab
Nahshon	Nahshon
Salmon	Salmon
Boaz	Boaz
Obed	Obed
Jesse	Jesse
David	David

Paternal Line

Maternal Line

Paternal Line	Maternal Line
Solomon	Nathan (Solomon's brother)
Rehoboam	Mattathah
Abijah	Menan
Asa	Melea
Jehoshaphat	Eliakim
Joram	Jonan
Uzziah	Joseph
Jotham	Judah
Ahaz	Simeon
Hezekiah	Levi
Manasseh	Matthat
Amon	Jorim
Josiah	Eliezer
Jeconiah	Jose
	Er
	Elmodam
	Cosam
	Addi
	Melchi
	Neri
Shealtiel } Intermarriage { Shealtiel	
Zerubbabel } Intermarriage { Zerubbabel	

Abiud ←—(Zerubbabel's sons)—→ Rhesa

Paternal Line	Maternal Line
Abiud	Rhesa
	Joannas
Eliakim	Judah
	Joseph
Azor	Semei
	Mattathiah
Zadok	Maath
	Naggai
Achim	Esli
	Nahum
Eliud	Amos
	Mattathiah
Eleazar	Joseph
	Janna
Matthan	Melchi
	Levi
Jacob	Matthat
	Heli
Joseph * Son-in-law to ——→	Mary

THE GENEALOGY OF JESUS ACCORDING TO MATTHEW AND LUKE

When one places the two genealogical lists side by side, there appear to be several conflicts in the accuracy of the lineage of Jesus. A careful look and a little understanding, explain the biblical discrepancies

1. Matthew reported the lineage of Christ only back to Abraham; Luke traced it all the way back to Adam.

2. Matthew used the expression "begat;" Luke used the expression "son of," which results in his list being a complete reversal of Matthew's.

3. The two genealogical lines parallel each other from Abraham to David.

4. Beginning with David, Matthew traced the **paternal** line of descent through Solomon; Luke traced the **maternal** line through Solomon's brother, Nathan.

5. The two lines (paternal and maternal) link together in the intermarriage of Shealtiel and Zerubbabel. But the linkage separates again in the two sons of Zerubbabel—Rhesa and Abiud.

6. The two lines come together once again for a final time in the marriage of Joseph and Mary. Joseph was the end of the **paternal** line, while Mary was the last of the **maternal** line as the daughter of Heli.

7. The reason Joseph is said to be the "son" of Heli (Mary's father) raises a question: the Jewish use of "son." Hebrews used the word in at least five distinct senses:

- ✡ in the sense used today of a one-generation offspring
- ✡ in the sense of a descendant, whether a grandson or a more remote descendant many generations previous, e.g., Matthew 1:1; 21:9; 22:42 ("begat" had this same flexibility in application)
- ✡ as a son-in-law—the Jews had no word to express this concept and so just used "son" e.g., 1 Samuel 24:16; 26:17
- ✡ in accordance with the Levirate marriage law—An **injunction that if a married man died without children**, it was the duty of a brother or other near relative to marry the widow, and the son of the union would be reckoned to be the son of the first husband (Deuteronomy 25:5-10).
- ✡ in the sense of a step-son who took on the legal status of his step-father—the relationship sustained by Jesus to Joseph (Matthew 13:55; Mark 6:3; Luke 3:23; 4:22; John 6:42).

Notice carefully that Joseph was a direct-line, blood descendant of David and, therefore, of David's throne. Here is the precise purpose of Matthew's genealogy: it demonstrated Jesus' **legal** right to inherit the throne of David—a necessary prerequisite to authenticating His Messianic claim. However, an equally critical credential was His **blood**/physical descent from David—a point that could not be established through Joseph since "after Jesus' mother Mary was betrothed to Joseph, before they came together, she was found with child **of the Holy Spirit**" (Matthew 1:18).

This feature of Christ's Messiahship was established through His mother Mary, who was also a blood descendant of David (Luke 1:30-32). Both the blood of David and the throne of David were necessary variables to qualify and authenticate Jesus as the Messiah.

THE VISION OF ABRAHAM

The almost incredible story of the Jews begins with a religious vision experienced by a seventy-five-year-old patriarch who lived about 2000 BC in the city of Ur. Ur was even then a very old city. It lay in the middle of the "cradle of civilization," the rich valley of Mesopotamia between the Tigris and Euphrates rivers.

The patriarch was Abraham. The little we know about him comes from the ancient family history recorded in Genesis, the first book of the Bible. But it is enough to establish him as a man of uncommon faith and courage.

Abraham lived in a polytheistic, idol-worshipping culture. According to Jewish tradition, he spent the first 40 years of his life questioning the polytheistic ideas of the surrounding culture, eventually concluding that all of existence comes from a single source—a primal infinite Being that we call God. Once he was confident in the truth of his theory, he began to publicize his ideas through writing, teaching, and public debates and eventually built a movement of tens of thousands of people committed to a belief in one Creator.

God put Abraham's faith to a severe test. "Go from your country and your kindred and your father's house to the land that I will show you," *He commanded, 'and I will make of you a great nation, and by you, all the families of the earth will be blessed.'" (Genesis 12:1)*

Abraham went. At an age when men are reluctant to risk new adventures, he pulled up stakes, severed all ties with home and family, and set forth with his wife Sarah for the Promised Land, then called Canaan, which later became known as Palestine. This act of obedience to God by an obscure man was one of the most important events in the religious history of humanity.

Abraham and Sarah were childless, and Sarah had already experienced menopause. She shrugged off with a bitter laugh Abraham's assurance that the Lord would make them the progenitors of a whole nation of people. But at the age of ninety, Sarah became pregnant and bore a son whom she named Isaac.

Isaac followed in his father's footsteps as a nomadic sheepherder. He had a son named Jacob. Jacob later acquired a new name, Israel; hence the terms "children of Israel," and "Israelites" for his descendants. (Genesis 32:29). Jacob's 12 sons were the kernels of 12 tribes that later developed into the Jewish nation. The name Jew derives from Judah one of the 12 sons of Jacob: Reuben, Simeon, Judah, Issachar, Zebulun, Benjamin, Dan, Naphtali, Gad, Asher, Ephraim, and Manasseh. (Exodus 1:1). So, the names Israel, Israeli or Jewish refer to people of the same origin.

In 1522 BC, during Jacob's old age, a severe famine drove his 70-member family out of Palestine and into Egypt. There the Israelites remained for several centuries (Genesis 46:8), where after 210 years (94 of them as slaves), they grew into a People of approximately 3 million. They clung doggedly to their separate philosophical, cultural, and linguistic identity, and continued to worship the God of Abraham, Isaac, and Jacob.

God chose a people through whom a Messiah could come.

"You Samaritans worship what you do not know; we worship what we do know, because salvation comes from the Jews." John 4:22. These were Jesus' very own words, all the blessings we have in Christ are first to be found in Abraham to whom God promised those blessings. And the promises of the Abrahamic Covenant have been entrusted to his descendants, the Jews. Without the Jews, we would have no patriarchs, no prophets, no apostles, no Bible and no Savior! Deprived of all these, how much salvation would we have left to us? None! **"....in thee (Abraham) shall all families of the earth be blessed." (Genesis 12:3.) "... in thee and in thy seed shall all the families of the earth be blessed." (Genesis 28:14) "Then what advantage has the Jew? What is the value of being circumcised? Much in every way! In the first place, the Jews were entrusted with the very words of God." (Romans 3:1-2)**

MOSES AND THE CHOSEN PEOPLE

The oppressed Israelites acquired a leader who, at the age of 80, was as full of faith and courage as his forefather Abraham. His name was Moses, one of the greatest leaders of all time. The second book of the Bible, Exodus, describes vividly how Moses led his people out of captivity with the help of "mighty acts of God." The pact, or covenant, that God had made with Abraham was renewed with Moses:

"If you will obey My voice and keep My covenant, you shall be My own possession among all peoples. You shall be to Me a kingdom of priests and a holy nation." (Exodus 19:3-8)

The Book of Exodus recounts how the Lord sent Moses to Pharaoh to serve as the deliverer of Israel. The Pharaoh, of course, refused Moses' appeal to set the Israelites free from their slavery, and the stage was then set for the showdown between the God of Israel and the so-called "gods" of Egypt. The final terrible plague that would descend upon the people of Egypt would be the death of the firstborn in the land. Only those families that sacrificed an unblemished male lamb and smeared its blood upon the doorposts of the house would be passed over from the impending wrath from heaven.

God commanded that on the 10th day of the Hebrew month of Nisan, each head of household should set aside a young male lamb to be examined for blemishes and to ensure its fitness as an offering. During the afternoon of the 14th, the lamb was slaughtered, and its blood smeared on all three sides of the doorframe, top, right and left.

On the 15th of Nisan, the meat of the Passover lamb was to be roasted and eaten with unleavened bread—matzah—and bitter herbs. The meal was to be eaten in haste since the Jews were to be ready to begin their journey immediately after God smote the firstborn. The Angel of Death *passed over* those homes whose doorposts were marked with the blood of the Passover lamb. God further commanded that Passover should be commemorated annually as a reminder of the deliverance from Egypt. Only unleavened bread is to be eaten for seven days, and the first and seventh days of Passover are to be days for holy assembly on which all work is forbidden.

The Israelites are led out of Egypt by Moses the Prophet in 1451 BC, and about 50 days later, find themselves awestruck at the foot of Mt Sinai, where God reveals Himself to the Nation as a whole, and proclaims the 10 Commandments. God seals a covenant with the Israelites, whereby they commit themselves (and their descendants) to follow the path of life which God will reveal for them (a path that would incorporate the philosophical system developed by Abraham). Moses then ascends Mt Sinai alone, and God teaches him all the details of that path. The enormous body of legal and moral principles revealed to Moses in the form of the Torah—the Five Books of Moses and the Oral laws found in the Mishna and Talmud (36 volumes).

Moses is hailed as the leader of the Exodus, the one through whom God delivered His people from Egyptian slavery. To Moses, God entrusted the Law. Moses is listed in Hebrews 11 as "exemplary of faith." In Deuteronomy 34 we read that God Himself buried Moses. We are also told, "since then, no prophet has risen in Israel like Moses, whom the Lord knew face to face. For no one has ever shown the mighty power or performed the awesome deeds that Moses did in the sight of all Israel" (Deuteronomy 34:10, 12). Yet Moses, for all his blessings, was not allowed to enter the Promised Land. Why not?

In Deuteronomy 32:51–52 God gives the reason that Moses was not permitted to enter the Promised Land: **because both of you broke faith with me among the Israelites at the waters of Meribah-Kadesh in the wilderness of Zin, by failing to maintain**

my holiness among the Israelites. Although you may view the land from a distance, you shall not enter it—the land that I am giving to the Israelites." God was true to His promise. He showed Moses the Promised Land but did not let him enter in.

The incident at the waters of Meribah-Kadesh is recorded in Numbers 20. Nearing the end of their forty years of wandering, the Israelites came to the Desert of Zin. There was no water, and the community turned against Moses and Aaron. Moses and Aaron went to the tent of meeting and prostrated themselves before God. God told Moses and Aaron to gather the assembly and speak to the rock. Water would come forth. Moses took the staff and gathered the men. Then, seemingly in anger, Moses said to them, "Listen, you rebels, must we bring you water out of this rock?" Then Moses struck the rock twice with his staff (Numbers 20:10–11). Water came from the rock, as God had promised. But God immediately told Moses and Aaron that, because they failed to trust Him enough to honor Him as holy, they would not bring the children of Israel into the Promised Land (verse 12).

The punishment may seem harsh to us, but, when we look closely at Moses' actions, we see several mistakes. Most obviously, Moses disobeyed a direct command from God. God had commanded Moses to speak to the rock. Instead, Moses struck the rock with his staff. Earlier, when God had brought water from a rock, He instructed Moses to strike it with a staff (Exodus 17). But God's instructions were different here. God wanted Moses to trust Him, especially after they had been in such a close relationship for so many years. Moses didn't need to use force; he simply needed to obey God and know that God would be true to His promise.

Also, Moses took the credit for bringing forth the water. He asks the people gathered at the rock, "Must *we* bring you water out of this rock?" (Numbers 20:10, emphasis added). Moses seemed to be taking credit for the miracle himself (and Aaron), instead of attributing it to God. Moses did this publicly. God could not let it go unpunished and expect the Israelites to understand His holiness.

The water-giving rock is used as a symbol of Christ in 1 Corinthians 10:4. The rock was struck in Exodus 17:6, just like Christ was crucified once (Hebrews 7:27). Moses' speaking to the rock in Numbers 20 could have been meant as a picture of prayer. Jesus was "struck" once, and He continues to provide living water to those who pray in faith to Him. When Moses angrily struck the rock, he destroyed the biblical typology and, in effect, crucified Christ again.

Moses' punishment for disobedience and pride was steep; he was barred from entering the Promised Land (Numbers 20:12). Yet we do not see Moses complain about his punishment. Instead, he continues to faithfully lead the people and honor God.

In His holiness, God is also compassionate. He invited Moses up to Mount Nebo where He showed His beloved prophet the Promised Land before his death. Deuteronomy 34:4–5 records, **"Then the Lord said to him, 'This is the land I promised on oath to Abraham, Isaac, and Jacob when I said, "I will give it to your descendants." I have let you see it with your eyes, but you will not cross over into it.' And Moses the servant of the Lord died there in Moab, as the Lord had said."** Moses' failure at the rock did not negate or break his relationship with God. God continued to use the prophet and continued to love him with tenderness.

The history of the Jews, recorded with such fascinating candor in the Old Testament, is that of a stiff-necked people who were always rebelling against the discipline of the Torah and turning their backs on God. They often resented the covenant, and instead of reveling in their unique role as a chosen people, wanted God to go away and leave them alone. God would not do that. Sometimes, when His chosen people grew particularly unruly, He would chastise them severely. Often, He sent prophets like Isaiah, Amos, and Jeremiah to castigate them for their willfulness and disobedience. But He never abandoned his covenant with them.

The Jews In Canaan

For several hundred years, the Land of Israel was organized into a confederacy of twelve tribes ruled by a series of Judges. After that came the Israelite monarchy, established in 1000 BC under Saul and continued under King David and his son, Solomon. During the reign of David, the already existing city of Jerusalem became the national and spiritual capital of the United Kingdom of Israel and Judah.

King Solomon built the First Temple on Mount Moriah in Jerusalem. However, the tribes were fracturing politically. Upon his death, a civil war erupted between the ten northern Israelite tribes, and the tribes of Judah (Simeon was absorbed into Judah) and Benjamin in the south. The nation split into the Kingdom of Israel in the north, and the Kingdom of Judah in the south. The Assyrian ruler Tiglath-Pileser III conquered the northern kingdom of Israel in the 8th century BC. No commonly accepted historical record accounts for the ultimate fate of the ten northern tribes, sometimes referred to as the Ten Lost Tribes of Israel, although speculation abounds.

About 1400 BC, after 40 years of traveling in the Sinai Desert, the Israelite Army, led by Joshua, conquers the Land of Canaan and inaugurates a period of over 1200 years of national experience in the Land of Israel, focused around the Jewish Temple in Jerusalem which existed for approximately 800 of those years (combining the 1st and 2nd Temple periods).

THE RULE OF ISRAEL

Babylonian Captivity (587–538 BC)

The year 587 BC marks a turning point in the history of the region. From this year onwards, the region was ruled or controlled by a succession of superpower empires of the time in the following order: Babylonian, Persian, Greek Hellenistic, Roman and Byzantine Empires, Islamic and Christian crusaders, Ottoman Empire, and the British Empire.

After revolting against the new dominant power and an ensuing siege, the Kingdom of Judah was conquered by the Babylonian army in 587 BC and the First Temple was destroyed. The elite of the kingdom and many of their people were exiled to Babylon, where the religion developed outside their traditional temple. Others fled to Egypt. After the fall of Jerusalem, Babylonia (modern-day Iraq), would become the focus of Judaism for more than a thousand years. The first Judahite communities in Babylonia started with the exile of the Tribe of Judah to Babylon by Jehoiachin in 597 BC as well as after the destruction of the Temple in Jerusalem in 586 BC. Babylonia, where some of the largest and most prominent Jewish cities and communities were established, became the center of Jewish life all the way up to the 13th century.

By the first century, Babylonia already held a speedily growing population of an estimated 1,000,000 Judahites which increased to an estimated 2 million between the years 200 AD and 500 AD, both by natural growth and by immigration of more Jews from the Land of Israel, making up about one-sixth of the world Jewish population at that era. It was there that they would write the Babylonian Talmud in the languages used by the Jews of ancient Babylonia—Hebrew and Aramaic.

After a few generations and with the conquest of Babylonia in 540 BC by the Persian Empire, some adherents led by prophets Ezra and Nehemiah returned to their homeland and traditional practices.

Post-Exilic Period (538–332 BC)

Following their return to Jerusalem after the return from the exile, and with Persian approval and financing, construction of the Second Temple was completed in 516 BC under the leadership of the last three Jewish Prophets Haggai, Zechariah, and Malachi.

After the death of the last Jewish prophet and while still under Persian rule, the leadership of the Jewish people passed into the hands of five successive generations of leaders. They flourished first under the Persians and then under the Greeks. As a result, the Pharisees and Sadducees were formed.

Hellenistic Period (c. 332–110 BC)

In 332 BC, the Persians were defeated by Alexander the Great of Macedonia. After his demise, and the division of Alexander's empire among his generals, the Seleucid Kingdom was formed.

Greek culture was spread eastwards by the Alexandrian conquests. During this time, currents of Judaism were influenced by Hellenistic philosophy developed from the 3rd century BC, notably the Jewish diaspora in Alexandria, culminating in the compilation of the Septuagint, the Greek translation of the Hebrew scriptures. An important advocate of the symbiosis of Jewish theology and Hellenistic thought was Philo, a Hellenistic Jewish philosopher.

The Hasmonean Kingdom (110–63 BC)

A deterioration of relations between Hellenized Jews and Orthodox Jews led the Seleucid king Antiochus IV Epiphanes to impose decrees banning certain Jewish religious rites and traditions.

Consequently, the Orthodox Jews revolted under the leadership of the Hasmonean family (also known as the Maccabees). This revolt eventually led to the formation of an independent Jewish kingdom, known as the Hasmonaean Dynasty, which lasted from 165 BC to 63 BC. The Hasmonean Dynasty eventually disintegrated as a result of civil war between the sons of Salome Alexandra.

Roman Rule in The Land of Israel (63 BC–324 AD)

Judea had been an independent Jewish kingdom under the Hasmoneans but was conquered by the Roman general Pompey in 63 BC and reorganized as a client state. Roman expansion was going on in other areas as well and would continue for more than a hundred and fifty years. Later, Herod the Great was appointed "King of the Jews" by the Roman Senate, supplanting the Hasmonean dynasty. Some of his offspring held various positions after him, known as the Herodian dynasty. Briefly, from 4 BC to 6 AD, Herod Archelaus ruled. The Romans denied him the title of King.

After the Census of Quirinius in 6 AD, the Roman province of Judaea was formed as a satellite of Roman Syria under the rule of a prefect until 41 AD, then procurators after 44 AD. The empire was often callous and brutal in its treatment of its Jewish subjects. In 30 AD (or 33 AD), Jesus of Nazareth, an itinerant rabbi from Galilee, and the central figure of Christianity, was put to death by crucifixion in Jerusalem under the Roman prefect of Judea, Pontius Pilate. In 66 AD, the Jews began to revolt against the Roman rulers of Judea. The revolt was defeated by the future Roman emperors Vespasian and Titus. In the Siege of Jerusalem in 70 AD, the Romans destroyed the Temple in Jerusalem and, according to some accounts, plundered artifacts from the temple, such as the Menorah.

JESUS OF NAZARETH: THE JEWISH PERSPECTIVE

From Jeremiah and other great prophets, the Jews learned that God would someday send a very special person—an "anointed one" (in Hebrew, *Mashiach,* "Messiah")—who, as their leader, would put everything right and establish the rule of God among all peoples. Anticipation of the Messiah's coming gradually developed into a major element of Jewish faith, a hope that sustained the Hebrews through hard times, exile, and suffering.

The story of Jesus has been recounted so often and so well in other books—and best of all in the New Testament—that it need not be repeated here in great detail. It is sufficient to note that he came from very humble origins—a carpenter's family in an obscure village; that he attracted no particular public attention during the first thirty years of his life; and that he then set forth to proclaim the advent of the "Kingdom of God"—the rule of God on earth which the prophets had said would be established by the Messiah.

There is no evidence that Jesus ever claimed to the crowds, in so many words, to be the Messiah. Perhaps he felt that the title had acquired too many connotations of earthly kingship. What he did say, boldly and repeatedly, was that he had been sent by "my Father in Heaven" to show men the way, to tell them the truth, and to make it possible for them to enter authentic, abundant life.

One of the certain facts about Jesus was that he was a Jew. He was a child of Jewish parents, brought up in a Jewish home and reared among Jewish traditions. Throughout his life, Jesus lived among Jews and his followers were Jews. Jesus and his family would have been observant of Torah, paid tithes, kept the Sabbath, circumcised their males, attended synagogue, observed purity laws in relation to childbirth and menstruation, kept the dietary code— and so on. While the Gospels record disputes about Jesus' interpretation of a few of these, the notion of a Christian Jesus, who did not live by Torah or only by its ethical values, does not fit historical reality.

Peter, James, John, and Paul were Jews. Yet we identify them with the "origins of Christianity." This is because we know that their efforts would eventually lead to the formation of that predominantly gentile religious community. But they did not know this! They foresaw no extended future.

They passionately believed that God was about to fulfill his ancient promises to Israel: to redeem history, to defeat evil, to raise the dead, and to establish a universal reign of justice and peace.

Their immediate source for this good news had been the prophecy of Jesus himself. And in their visions of Jesus resurrected, his followers' hopes were confirmed: Jesus' own resurrection could only mean that the general resurrection —thus, the coming of God's Kingdom—truly was at hand. Now linking the Kingdom's imminent arrival to the victorious return of their Messiah, these followers raced to proclaim the good news in what they were sure was a brief wrinkle in time, the Spirit-charged gap between the raising of Jesus and his glorious second coming.

No other Jew in history has rivalled Jesus in the magnitude of his influence. The words and deeds of Jesus the Jew have been, and are, an inspiration to countless millions of men and women.

There is no official Jewish view of Jesus but in one respect Jews are agreed in their attitude towards Jesus. Jews reject the tremendous claim, which is made for Jesus by his Christian followers—that Jesus is the Lord Christ, God Incarnate, the very Son of God the Father. On that belief, Jews and Christians must continue to respectfully differ. Jews believe that all share the divine spirit and are stamped with the divine image and no person—not even the greatest of all people—can possess the perfection of God. No one can be God's equal.

Jesus lived his life not as a Christian but as a Jew, obedient (with very few exceptions) to Torah. Yet within a few years after his death, the Jewish followers of Jesus espoused a rather different kind of religion from that followed by most Jews. Judaism, like Islam after it, is strongly rooted in religious law; Christianity ceased to be so. Judaism, also like Islam, has a strong belief in the unity of God; Christianity came to place such great store in Jesus and subsequently in the doctrine of the Trinity that it has seemed to many other monotheists to be a refined form of polytheism. Gradually, Christian religion came to look less like an authentic form of Judaism, and more like a completely different religion.

Jesus was put to death by the Romans on the charge that he claimed to be the Messiah. Jesus made it clear to Peter that he regarded himself as the Messiah *"But what about you?" he asked. "Who do you say I am?" Peter answered, "You are the Messiah." (Mark 8:29)* as he did to the High Priest, *"I am," said Jesus. "And you will see the Son of Man sitting at the right hand of the Mighty One and coming on the clouds of heaven." (Mark 14:62).* Some Jews accepted Jesus as Messiah, believing that he would redeem them from the bitter yoke of Rome and bring the messianic age. When Jesus rode into Jerusalem he was acclaimed, *"blessed is the Kingdom that comes, the kingdom of our father David" (Mark 11:10).* Other Jews rejected the claim.

During the Second Temple period, there were many internal arguments about what it meant to be Jewish. Did religious law permit one to acquiesce in Roman occupation, or to fight it? How did the law reconcile justice and mercy? These must have been common debates, which one can see mirrored in the gospels' accounts of Jesus' disputes with contemporary religious leaders.

We cannot be certain of Jesus' views, for the gospels are a highly interpretative chronicle of events that had happened 40 and more years before. Even so, His attitude towards dietary laws recorded in Mark's gospel shows little interest in the minutiae of what they require that Jews eat and drink. This unusual interpretation eventually became common for Christians: certainly, the food laws, for Christians, gradually became a thing of the past, as accounts in Acts and the Pauline letters illustrate. Moreover, although Jesus' message of the Kingdom of God was clearly within mainstream Jewish tradition, the Christological references about him and his meaning are less so.

The belief that Jesus was God is an impossibility for Jewish thought. But not so the belief that Jesus claimed to be the Messiah. Several Jews have in the course of 2000 years, claimed to be the Messiah—sent by God to inaugurate God's kingdom on earth. Simon Bar Kochba in 132 AD and Shabbetai Zvi in 1665 AD are two examples among many. But the association of Messiah with terms like Son of Man and Son of God, which developed a profusion of meanings, soon led to exalted claims for Jesus that few Jews felt able to follow. Even within the New Testament this is so; by the time of the full-blown Trinitarianism of the 4th century, this gap was impossibly wide.

The charge against Jesus on the cross and his mockery as 'King of the Jews', his execution between two villains, the appearance of the royal messianic motifs—these all suggest that Pilate faced a man charged with sedition. Jesus was not crucified because he denied his Jewishness, abandoned the Scriptures, or disowned his people.

He remained a Jew, Jesus of Nazareth, the Jew from Galilee and was executed for political rather than religious reasons.

To claim to be the Messiah, if it was an offense against Judaism at all, was certainly not (as the Gospels contend) an offense against Jewish law for which Jesus could have been put to death. The Gospels say that Jesus' claim to be the Messiah was blasphemy, but in Jewish law, blasphemy was to curse God using God's sacred name. Jesus did nothing of the sort. For Jews, history has shown that Jesus was not the long-awaited Messiah, for Jews were not delivered from the yoke of Roman bondage and the Golden Age did not come. However, some Jews have suggested that Jesus was following in the footsteps of the biblical prophets, *"He said to them, go into all the world and preach the gospel to all creation. Whoever believes and is baptized will be saved, but whoever does not believe will be condemned." (Mark 6:15-16).*

"What commandment is the first of all?" he was asked. Jesus answered as any Jew: "the first is: Hear O Israel the Lord our God, the Lord is One. And you shall love the Lord your God with all your heart, with all your soul and with all your might. (Deuteronomy 6:4-9) The second is this: You shall love your neighbor as yourself. There is no other commandment greater than these." (Mark 12:28-31).

Every Jew will recognize in Jesus' answer the **Shema (Deuteronomy 6:4-9)**, a Jewish declaration of faith, which is recited at every Jewish service, day and night. The famous command, *"You shall not take vengeance or bear a grudge against any of your people, but you shall love your neighbor as yourself: I am the LORD." (Leviticus 19:18)* is also a fundamental precept of Judaism.

It was in his attitude towards the Torah that Jesus seems to have departed from the Judaism of his time. In their teaching, the rabbis would state, "thus says the Torah." Jesus showed independence by standing above the Torah and speaking. *"The people were amazed at his teaching, because he taught them as one who had authority, not as the teachers of the law." (Mark 1:22)* He dared to base his teachings on "I say to you" and it was this daring which brought him into conflict with contemporary Judaism.

It is highly improbable that Jesus told his followers to ignore the Torah; rather, he emphasized that *"the Kingdom of God is within you" (Luke 17:21)* i.e., follow the deepest instinct for truth and love in your heart for therein, not through Torah, lies salvation. This was a courageous message; one which made some Jews unbounded in their devotion to him and others to regard him as a heretic.

At least until the 1970s, it was common for New Testament scholars to portray Jesus as a kind of prototype exponent of idealism. Many betrayed an instinctive antisemitism. They depicted Judaism at the time of Jesus as 'late Judaism', as if the Jewish religion had ended with the destruction of the Temple in 70 AD—or should have. This position was based on the conviction that post-exilic Judaism had betrayed the prophetic faith of Israel. It contends that Jesus stands outside such a hardened, legalistic religion, a stranger to it, condemning the scribes and the Pharisees who were the fathers of Rabbinic Judaism and who have thus misled modern Judaism into perpetuating this sterile, legalistic religion.

Jesus was a Jew, not an alien intruder in 1st-century Palestine. Whatever else he was, he was a reformer of Jewish beliefs, not an indiscriminate fault-finder of them. For Jews, the significance of Jesus must be in his life rather than his death, a life of faith in God. For Jews, not Jesus but God alone is Lord. Yet an increasing number of Jews are proud that Jesus was born, lived and died a Jew.

JUDAISM IN THE TIME OF JESUS

Scholars estimate that approximately 4,000,000 Jews lived in the Roman Empire during the first century. As a result of war, exile, trade, and business the Jews were dispersed throughout the Empire. The Jews of the Dispersion, designated Diaspora, practiced the same religion but at the same time were distinct from the Jews in Judea. They spoke Greek while the Jews of Judea usually spoke Hebrew or Aramaic. As a result, the Diaspora read the Scriptures in Greek, the Septuagint, and not the Hebrew. In general, the Jews separated themselves religiously and morally from the influences of other cultures, but other areas of their lives were affected by living in areas where they were in the minority.

Jewish society was generally less stratified than the rest of the Roman world. Chief priests and rabbis formed the upper class. Most of the population was farmers, artisans, or small businessmen. Tax collectors were despised because of their immorality. The Roman government assigned these jobs to the individual who would do the job for the lowest pay. They would then collect taxes illegally and keep them thus making a living for themselves.

Jewish families were usually large. Boys were more valued than girls were. Families had no last names and therefore were identified by their father, their occupation, their political position, or where they were from. Jews ate only two meals a day, one at midday and the other at night. They ate mostly fruit and vegetables; consuming meat only on special occasions.

Many people converted to Judaism. Godfearers were those individuals who practiced elements of the religion but were not circumcised and did not fully follow the law. The Jews expected a Messiah, and most believed that he would come in the form of a prophet, a priest, or a royal official. It is important to understand that they expected a human, not a divine being to come and save them from Rome. There were also those who proposed that God would deliver His people and then set up a ruler who would reign over them.

Although at the beginning of the Christian era Judaism comprised of several different groups: the Pharisees, the Sadducees, the Essenes, the Zealots—and those who followed Jesus, the Nazarenes. In spite of differences between them, the groups were united by certain basic beliefs: belief in one God, belief in the covenant which God had made with his people Israel, and belief in the foundational book of this covenant, the Law of God or the Torah.

The covenant between God and Israel covered duties and commitments which pertained to both parties. God committed himself to treat Israel in accordance with its special position as his own people, and to teach the Israelites the principles of a good and blessed life. Israel made the commitment to be obedient to God and to live a life befitting the people of God. These principles are found in the Torah or Law of Moses, its teaching and practical applications. The Torah also included directions concerning atonement for offenses committed so that the covenant might nevertheless remain in effect.

It is important to note that in Judaism the Law is not a way of salvation. Salvation—the election of God—is based exclusively on the grace of God.

The Temple

The Temple was the most important symbol of the Jewish people, the center of life, where the national, the cultural, the religious and the political were fused.

The first Jerusalem Temple was built by King Solomon. The Babylonians destroyed it in 587 BC. At the same time the upper classes of the kingdom of Judah were exiled to Babylon. After conquering the Babylonian Empire, Cyrus, the king of Persia, granted the Jews permission to return to their homeland and build a new temple. Five hundred years later King Herod initiated a massive rebuilding project, the aim of which was to restore the splendor of Solomon's Temple. The Temple was dedicated in 18 BC, but the project was only completed in the 60s AD Its size and beauty were widely known, but it was destroyed in the turmoil of the Jewish War in 70 AD

A new temple could no longer be built because the Jews were expelled from Palestine half a century later. Today the site is occupied by mosques, so both archaeological excavations and the construction of a new temple are impossible. All that remains is a western section of the Temple wall, commonly known as the 'Wailing Wall'.

The outer court of Herod's Temple was called the 'Court of the Gentiles'. Inside it was the Temple area, divided off by a wall, to which all but Jews were forbidden entry on pain of death. The outer part of the Temple area proper was the 'Court of the Women', then the 'Court of the Men'. Only priests were permitted to proceed further, to the altar. On this altar were performed the daily animal sacrifices.

The inner vestibule of the Temple was called 'holy'. Here were the seven-branched candlestick, the table of the shewbread and the altar. The 'holy' was divided from the 'holy of holies' by a curtain, inside which the high priest could go once a year, on the Day of Atonement, to offer a sacrifice for the whole people.

In the outmost court of the Temple were traders, from whom pilgrims who had travelled from afar might purchase sacrificial animals. The money-changers exchanged foreign currency for silver shekels, with which the Temple tax and the price of the sacrificial animal were paid.

In the Temple area was also the Antonia Fortress, one of Herod's palaces, which was in the north-west corner of the area. From the fortress it was possible to maintain order in the Temple, especially during Passover. It may have been in the Antonia Fortress that Pontius Pilate sentenced Jesus to be crucified.

In the Temple there served both priests and Levites. The latter did not participate in the sacrificial cult but took care of the music, guarding and cleaning of the Temple.

The Temple Sacrifices

The priests offered numerous sacrifices in the Temple every day, since the Law of Moses obliged Jews to purify themselves and atone for their sins by offering a sacrifice. In addition, thanksgiving offerings were sacrificed. The victim might be a sheep or a dove; flour and wine might also be offered as a sacrifice. In addition to the sacrifices brought by individuals, communal sacrifices were offered every day in the Temple.

An example of the sacrifice of a sheep: The animal's throat was slit, and the blood was collected in a bowl for throwing on the altar. The animal was skinned, and the fat was burnt in the fire on the altar. The hide and part of the meat was put to one side, for the priests gained their living from the sacrifices during their term of service in the Temple. The rest of the meat was given to the person who brought the offering. He left the Temple to eat it with his friends and family.

A burnt offering was an offering which was burnt whole in the fire on the altar (the blood and hide were removed before the offering was burnt). Because the sacrificial animal had to be flawless, it was most convenient to buy it in the Temple. The pilgrim who came from afar took a substantial risk in bringing the sacrificial victim with him, for it might injure itself on the journey and no longer be fit to be sacrificed.

The Pharisees—In the Gospels the Pharisees often appear as the influential arch-enemies of Jesus. They tirelessly watch how the Jewish people observe the purity and holiness code. From this the word 'Pharisee' has come commonly to be a synonym of 'hypocrite'. Such a picture of the Pharisees is, however, one-sided. In fact, the Pharisees were one Jewish group among many - a lay movement which placed emphasis on the Torah (the Law of Moses and its interpretation) and, in particular on the importance of the purity code for everyday holiness.

There were also many different types of Pharisee. Some of them seem to have been close to Jesus in their thinking. Sayings resembling the teaching of Jesus occur among the sayings of Rabbi Hillel, for instance, and Hillel was active in Pharisaic circles. The Apostle Paul also came from among the Pharisees.

In the opinion of the Pharisees holiness was not only for the priests and the Temple. By observing the purity code every member of the people of God might participate in the holiness of God. In the interpretation of the written Law the Pharisees had the help of the so-called 'Oral Law', i.e. oral tradition consisting of explanations of the Law which was thought to go back to Moses himself.

Conflicts between the Pharisees and the disciples of Jesus came to a head after the death of Jesus, when the Jesus movement began to accept Gentiles into membership without demanding that they be circumcised or that they observe the purity code. These controversies are reflected in the way the Pharisees are portrayed in the New Testament.

Another group often mentioned in the New Testament in connection with the Pharisees are the Teachers of the Law. Here we are dealing with a very different group of people. While the Pharisees were a kind of revival movement, 'Teacher of the Law' is a professional term. The Teachers of the Law were authoritative professional interpreters of the Torah.

The Sadducees—Only sparse information has been preserved concerning the Sadducees, and none of it is impartial; most of the information comes from their opponents. In the traditional view the Sadducees were from the Hellenized Jewish upper class, which supported stable conditions and the prevailing social order, and whose religion was reasonable and worldly. The Sadducees did not, for example, believe in life after death.

The name of the Sadducees is believed to derive from the family of Zadok, the high priest who served as high priest in the days of King David. Not all the Sadducees were priests, however, and their number included other aristocrats. On the other hand, evidently only a small minority of the upper class were Sadducees.

The Essenes—The Essenes are not mentioned in the New Testament; the information concerning them is derived from other sources. Since 1947, manuscript and archaeological discoveries have been made at Qumran and they are thought to derive from the Essenes who dwelt there. The Essenes were a protest movement which withdrew from the world. They believed that the high priest of the Jerusalem Temple was elected on false pretenses, which invalidated the whole Temple cult. In addition, the calendar used by the Essenes and their way of interpreting and observing the Law of Moses differed from the rest of Judaism.

The Essene community of Qumran saw itself as the only true Israel, "children of light" as distinct from the "children of darkness" and their corrupt religious practices. The members of the community lived a disciplined life dictated by the regulations and a strict system of values. At the same time, they like many of their contemporaries, expected that God would soon intervene in the course of history in a decisive manner.

The Dead Sea Scrolls were discovered in eleven caves along the northwest shore of the Dead Sea between the years 1947 and 1956. The area is 13 miles east of Jerusalem and is 1300 feet below sea level. The mostly fragmented texts are numbered according to the cave that they came out of. They have been called the greatest manuscript discovery of modern times.

Although the Qumran community existed during the time of the ministry of Jesus, none of the Scrolls refer to Him, nor do they mention any of His followers described in the New Testament.

The Dead Sea Scrolls enhance our knowledge of both Judaism and Christianity. They represent a non-rabbinic form of Judaism and provide a wealth of comparative material for New Testament scholars, including many important parallels to the Jesus movement. They show Christianity to be rooted in Judaism and have been called the evolutionary link between the two.

Some of the manuscripts were carefully packed in clay jars; most, however, were lying on the floors of the caves, at the mercy of damp and worms. The manuscripts were evidently concealed in the caves for fear of discovery by Roman soldiers. The Roman army destroyed the settlement in 68 AD.

The last words of Joseph, Judah, Levi, Naphtali, and Amram (the father of Moses) are written down in the Scrolls. The story of Abraham includes an explanation why God asked Abraham to sacrifice his only son Isaac.

The Scrolls are most commonly made of animal skins, but also papyrus and the most curious one of copper. The Copper Scroll, discovered in Cave 3, records a list of 64 underground hiding places throughout the land of Israel. The deposits are to contain certain amounts of gold, silver, aromatics, and manuscripts. These are believed to be treasures from the Temple at Jerusalem, that were hidden away for safekeeping.

The oldest manuscripts found at Qumran were fragments of Old Testament manuscript copies from the third century BC Most of the manuscripts, however, date from the two centuries preceding the turn of the era and the first century following it, that is, the time when the group that wrote and copied the scrolls lived at Qumran.

In all scholars have identified the remains of about 825 to 870 separate scrolls. The scrolls can be divided into two categories— biblical and non-biblical. Fragments of every book of the Hebrew canon have been discovered except for the book of Esther. There are now identified among the scrolls, 19 copies of the Book of Isaiah, 25 copies of Deuteronomy and 30 copies of Psalms. The Isaiah Scroll found relatively intact is 100 years older than any previously known copy of Isaiah. In fact, the scrolls are the oldest group of Old Testament manuscripts ever found.

Before the discovery of these scrolls, the oldest complete copy of the Old Testament in Hebrew was Codex Babylonicus Petropalitanus (housed in Leningrad) from 1008 AD, more than 1400 years after the Old Testament was completed.

If the Masoretic version is the one and only true Old Testament, then the Dead Sea Scrolls are extremely good news for Bible believers, Jewish or Christian. The Masoretic manuscripts among the Dead Sea Scrolls are astonishingly similar to the standard Hebrew texts 1,000 years later, proving that Jewish scribes were accurate in preserving and transmitting the Masoretic Scriptures.

The Dead Sea Scrolls demonstrated unequivocally the fact that the Jews were faithful in their transcription of biblical manuscripts. This reverence for the Scriptures was summed up long ago by the first century Jewish historian, Flavius Josephus: "We have given practical proof of our reverence for our own Scriptures. For, although such long ages have now passed, no one has ventured either to add, or to remove, or to alter a syllable; and it is an instinct with every Jew from the day of his birth to regard them as the decrees of God, to abide by them, and, if need be, cheerfully die for them." *(Josephus, Complete Works, translated by William Whiston, Grand Rapids, Kregel 1960)*

The Zealots—The Zealots were a group of Jewish nationalists who strongly opposed Roman rule. The Zealot movement stemmed from the action of Judah the Galilean, who believed theocracy should be the law of the land and Jews should not pay tribute to Rome nor acknowledge the emperor as their master. Judah was apparently killed in the suppression of this revolt. His followers took to the deserts, where they maintained a guerrilla resistance against the Romans.

One of Christ's apostles, Simon, was a Zealot (Luke 6:15), indicating that Zealot principles were not inconsistent with the church. Christ was later associated with Zealot activities at his Roman trial when his fate was linked with that of Barabbas, who had led a recent insurrection against the Romans. (Mark 15:7.)

The Zealots increased their activities in the years following Christ's death, seizing the temple in 66 AD. The Romans forcibly crushed this revolt and destroyed Jerusalem (and the Temple) in 70 AD Shortly after this, the Zealots made their last and fateful stand against Roman rule as they defended their garrison at Masada, a desert plateau near the Dead Sea, holding off the Roman army for over a year. Ultimately the Jews at Masada committed suicide rather than surrender to the Romans.

The Jewish Diaspora

Diaspora means "dispersion". The term was used to describe Jewish communities living outside Palestine. The Jewish diaspora began with the Assyrian conquest and continued on a much larger scale with the Babylonian conquest, in which the Tribe of Judah was exiled to Babylonia along with the dethroned King of Judah, Jehoiachin, in the 6th century BC, and was taken into captivity in 597 BC. The exile continued after the destruction of Solomon's Temple in Jerusalem in 586 BC.

Many of the Judaean Jews were sold into slavery while others became citizens of other parts of the Roman Empire. The Book of Acts in the New Testament, as well as other Pauline texts, make frequent reference to the large populations of Hellenized Jews in the cities of the Roman world. These Hellenized Jews were affected by the diaspora only in its spiritual sense, absorbing the feeling of loss and homelessness that became a cornerstone of the Jewish identity, much supported by persecutions in various parts of the world. The policy encouraging proselytism and conversion to Judaism, which spread the Jewish religion throughout the Hellenistic civilization, seems to have subsided with the wars against the Romans.

Of critical importance to the reshaping of Jewish tradition from the Temple-based religion to the rabbinic traditions of the Diaspora, was the development of the interpretations of the Torah found in the *Mishnah* and *Talmud.*

At the beginning of the Christian era there were Jews living all over the Roman Empire and in the East beyond the frontiers of the Empire. They lived in the country and in the towns, and they came from all social classes and professions. Their customs were known everywhere, even if they were not always regarded favorably. On the other hand, their strict monotheism and high moral standards attracted many, and they often had influential patrons.

Sometimes non-Jews joined the Jewish community. Those who converted and became full members were called proselytes. Becoming a member was preceded by ritual purification (immersion in the **Mikveh**) and in the case of male proselytes by circumcision. At the same time the newcomers committed themselves to observing the commands of the Torah. This was a great deal to ask, and the number of proselytes remained small.

"God-fearers" was the name for non-Jews who instead of becoming proselytes were satisfied with observing the Jewish way of life and taking part in the life of the Jewish community as far as it was possible. This group later become fertile ground for early Christian missionary work.

The synagogue represented the center of Jewish worship. The synagogue was rectangular in shape with a speaker's platform. Behind the platform stood a chest in which the Old Testament scrolls were stored. People sat on mats, stone benches, or wooden chairs. The rulers and priests sat opposite the congregation facing them. The people sang without music. The speaker stood to read from the Old Testament scrolls and sat down after he taught from them. Everyone stood during prayer. Animal sacrifices were only offered in the Jerusalem Temple. The synagogue became the center of all Jewish life including a place for political meetings, a school for Jewish children, and a courtroom.

Diaspora Jews also met in synagogues, the size and manner of construction of which depended on the resources of the community. In large towns, there might be several. The head of the synagogue was the spiritual leader and senior teacher of the community. Temporal matters were looked after by the council of elders, the secretary acting as bookkeeper and correspondent. The synagogue servant was responsible for maintaining the property and for keeping order and if necessary, he led the prayers.

Besides being a place of worship, the synagogue had a Torah school. The synagogue also functioned as a communal meeting-place and as somewhere where people from various professions could meet.

Exile and Return

In 70 AD the Roman army destroys the Second Temple, the first was destroyed by the Babylonians about 500 years earlier, and from this point onwards, most Jews live in various communities outside the Land of Israel. For the next 1900 years, the Jews in exile pray 3 times daily to be able to return to their homeland and in 1948 the dream is realized with a majority vote in the United Nations to allow the re-establishment of a Jewish State in the Land of Israel.

The people of modern-day Israel share the same language and culture shaped by the Jewish heritage and religion passed through generations starting with the founding father Abraham (ca. 1800 BC). Thus, Jews have had a continuous presence in the land of Israel for the past 3,300 years.

JEWISH BELIEFS

In Abraham's time, the Jews were just a tribe, a band of nomads, probably shepherds. Had they remained merely shepherds, they would have eventually died out, one of the many tiny "nations" to be found in the ancient Near East, forgotten by all but the archaeologists.

But the Jews became something more. They were the bearers of a radically new concept, **ethical monotheism.** That concept became the basis for a new kind of religion, Judaism—marked by a new relationship between people and their Deity.

Contemporary scholars suggest that—at least at the start—the Hebrews believed in their own God, acknowledging the existence of other people's gods, but they also believed that their God could beat up everyone else's gods. Scripture tends to confirm that view; in Exodus 12:12, Adonai tells Moses, **"Against all the gods of Egypt I will exercise judgments."**

This much seems clear: the idea of a single, omnipotent, omniscient God is a Jewish invention, one that has changed the course of Western (and, therefore, world) history. Let's begin with that concept and the ways in which it marks the Jewish religion. The Jewish idea of the relationship between God and humanity is perhaps nowhere clearer than in Jewish prayer, so it is there that we turn.

The essential belief that all recognize as coming to Christianity through the Jewish people is the belief in one God. After the fall of Jerusalem and the destruction of the Temple in 70 AD, early Christians were persecuted for not worshipping the many Roman gods.

In other early belief systems, the ones that we casually denote as "pagan," divine creatures predate the creation of the world and humanity; but these belief systems have creation myths that usually involve the creation of the gods themselves. The opening words of the Hebrew Bible—***Bereshit bara Elohim…In the beginning, God created***…offer a very different vision. God is a given, a Being who creates out of chaos and nothingness, a Being who pre-exists Creation, who was, is, and always will be.

At the heart of Jewish prayer is the idea that God listens to prayer, that prayers are part of a dialogue between man and Creator. This idea has its roots in the Hebrew Bible itself, implicit in the statement that man was created in the image of God.

THE NAMES OF GOD

The God of the Hebrew Bible has many names, one of which is never pronounced.

The Jewish God is not merely a philosophical concept, a final cause that explains the existence of the universe. He is a personal

God, the true hero of the biblical stories, and the guide and mentor of His Chosen People. As such He has a proper name. In the Hebrew scriptures, that name is written as: יהוה

Hebrew script originally contained no vowels. God's name was almost certainly pronounced in early times, but by the third century BC, the consonants were regarded as so sacred that they were never articulated. Instead, the convention was to read the letters as **Adonai,** which means "Lord." Thus, in English transliterations of the Hebrew text is JHWH and is never written as a proper name, but as "the Lord."

יהוה is explained in the book of Exodus as "I am Who I am."

The term "Jehovah" was introduced by Christian scholars. It is merely JHWH pronounced with the vowel of Adonai, thus making JeHoWaH. It is a hybrid and is ***not*** usually used by Jews.

For non-Jews, the most familiar name derived from the Hebrew Bible is probably Jehovah, a mis-transliteration of the four-letter name, Yud-Hay-Vav-Hay, the Tetragrammaton.

Over the course of time, even the title Adonai was regarded as too awesome to represent the four letters of God's name and today most Orthodox Jews use the term HaShem, which simply means "the Name."

Terms for God are treated with the greatest reverence. Among the strictly traditional, even English translations are perceived as too holy to write and today the custom is to inscribe God, the Lord, and even the Almighty. This carefulness is explained and justified by the prohibition in the Ten Commandments: "You shall not take the name of your God in vain; for Adonai will not hold him guiltless who takes His name in vain" (Exodus 20:7).

God has many names in the Hebrew scriptures and in Jewish liturgy. The Holy One tells Moses, *I revealed Myself to Abraham, to Isaac, and to Jacob as El Shaddai, but my name Adonai I did not make known to them." (Exodus 6:3)*

In the Bible and the Talmud, God has many more names:

Elohim—God	This name refers to God's incredible power and might. He is the one and only God. He is supreme.
El Elyon—God Most High	This means God Most High. It is a name that is used through the Old Testament revealing God is above all gods, that nothing in life is more sacred.
El Shaddai— God Almighty	Psalm 91:1 He who dwells in the shelter of the Most High will rest in the shadow of the Almighty.
El Olam— God Everlasting	El is another name that is translated as God—Olam literally means forever, eternity, everlasting. When combined it can be translated as Eternal God or God Everlasting
Adon, Adonai— Lord, Master	Adon is singular, Adonai is plural. When referring to God, the plural is used. When Adon is used it refers to a human lord.
Shekinah	The Glorified Countenance of God

Many traditionally observant Jews will not write the vernacular equivalent of the sacred names, preferring *G-d* or *L-rd*. Contrary to popular belief, this practice does not come from the commandment not to take God's name in vain. Judaism does not prohibit writing the name of God. But it does prohibit erasing or defacing the name of God. Consequently, observant Jews avoid writing any name of God casually because of the risk that the written name might later be defaced, obliterated, or destroyed accidentally or by one who does not know better.

This prohibition applies only to Names that are written in some permanent form. Recent rabbinical decisions have held that typing on a computer is not a permanent form, thus it is not a violation to type God's name into a computer and then backspace over it or cut and paste it or copy and delete files with God's name in them. However, once you print the document out, it becomes "permanent."

Old, worn, or damaged Torahs, prayer books and other ritual objects must be collected and buried in a Jewish cemetery. Study materials may be put in an envelope and recycled.

THE SACRED TEXTS

What is the difference between Torah, Tanakh, Talmud, Midrash, Mishnah, and other similar terms?

The Torah—is the first 5 books (Genesis, Exodus, Leviticus, Numbers, and Deuteronomy) of the Tanakh. "Torah" means "law" or "instruction" in Hebrew, and accordingly, the Torah documents the laws given to Moses on Mt Sinai by God, for the Jewish people.

The Tanakh—is the "Hebrew Bible" or "Masoretic (Hebrew) Old Testament" (only with a slight variation in the order of books). The word "TaNaKh" is a Hebrew acronym which describes how the book's content is split into three categories:

Ta = Torah = Law
Na = Nevi'im = Prophets
Kh = Ketuvim = Writing

While the Torah is the law that governs the lives of the Jews, the Nevi'im and Ketuvim were written so the reader could better understand the nature of God.

The Mishnah—The Mishnah is the "Oral Torah". Exodus 24:12 says that God told Moses "I will give you the stone tablets with the teachings *and* commandments". Mainstream Judaism interprets this to mean that God gave Moses commandments that were not written in the Torah, but rather spoken to him and passed down through the generations by spoken word. As an example, Exodus 12:2 doesn't clarify which calendar to use. In the 2nd Century AD, these laws were written down and preserved in The Mishnah.

The Gemara—In the following centuries, the Rabbinical discussions and debates regarding the interpretation of the Mishnah are recorded.

The Talmud—is the compiled record of the Mishnah and the Gemara.

Midrash—is a form of rabbinic commentary and interpretation that attempts to clarify ambiguities in the original ancient text, or to make the words used applicable to current times. They are often metaphorical or allegorical in nature. Sometimes, the Mishnah or the entire Talmud is referred to as "Midrash" because of their structure and purpose as bodies of text.

There are two types of Midrashic writings:

Midrash Halacha = literature that attempts to clarify ambiguities in the text regarding legal issues. For example, whether tefillin are used during prayer and how they should be worn.

Midrash Aggadah (also spelled Haggadah) = literature that consists of wisdom and teachings, stories, and parables. For example, why Adam did not stop Eve from consuming the Garden of Eden's forbidden fruit.

THREE MOVEMENTS

It is true that the major movements that characterize organized Jewish religious life in the West today are creations of the modern era. But it is also true that throughout Jewish history, there have been different factions and different interpretations of the law.

During the Second Temple era, three distinct groups—the Pharisees, Sadducees, and Essenes—had varied understandings of the law and also constituted different social classes. And when the Hasidic movement emerged in Eastern Europe in the 18th century, its emphasis on religious "experience" over textual study, and individual communities' allegiance to charismatic rebbes, created significant tension with the dominant traditional rabbinical leadership.

Yet the Jews have managed to avoid the kind of schisms that led to a decisive split, never creating what would be in effect a new religion. (Possible exceptions to this were the Samaritans and the Karaites, but both groups emerged before the existence of rabbinical Judaism as we know it today.)

The Jewish movements are known as Reform, Conservatism and Orthodoxy, which are—in that order—the largest organized groups in the United States and to a lesser extent outside it, came into existence among Ashkenazi Jews in Central Europe in the early 19th century. (Sephardic Jews, the descendants of those exiled from Iberia, the southwest corner of Europe, beginning in 1492 and of Jews from North Africa and the Middle East, have for the most part remained traditional in observance and not been drawn to these modern movements.)

The Reform and Conservative movements developed out of the Enlightenment and the Jewish Emancipation in the 18th century. The first was the intellectual upheaval revolution that led to the scientific revolution and to the concepts of tolerance and human rights; the latter saw the Jews of individual states being granted civil rights like other citizens. Together, these developments allowed Jews to leave their ghettos, acquire secular education and, at least to some extent, integrate into Christian society. Inevitably, many of these same Jews began to subject their tradition and texts to a critical approach, while the opportunity to join secular society led some to adjust their dress and their lifestyle so as to fit in.

Reform Judaism was the most radical development. It rejected the idea of the Torah (meaning, Jewish law in general) being divinely written, but rather saw it as being composed by a variety of different sources over time. It also rejected the binding nature of halakha (religious law) and dispensed with those practices that did not seem to embody ethical values and teachings.

Today, Reform is the largest movement in the United States, and internationally, under the rubric of Progressive Judaism, it claims some 1.7 million members. In recent years, many Reform synagogues have moved back toward tradition, but the ideology remains the same. The movement is egalitarian, in many countries sanctifies same-sex unions, and it gives members the maximum freedom to decide on their own level of observance.

Probably the most significant innovation of American Reform Judaism was the decision, in 1983, to recognize patrilineal lineage in additional to matrilineal. This means that the movement accepts as Jewish anyone with either a Jewish mother or father. Since this contradicts Jewish religious law, which also forbids intermarriage, it runs the risk of creating a class of people who define themselves as Jewish but who are not seen as such by the majority of the world's Jews.

Conservative Judaism was a reaction to Reform. Although it agreed that Scripture and other essential texts were drafted by humans, it saw them as being divinely inspired, with their principles and laws coming from God. Consequently, it also saw Jews as being bound by religious law, even as it suggested that the law had always been subject to—and should continue as such into the present—human interpretation and adaptation to cultural circumstances.

On the practical level, there is often a gap between the observance level of Conservative rank-and-file and the nominally binding religious rulings of their leadership.

In the United States, about one-quarter of all Jews define themselves as Conservative Jews and has some 900 synagogues affiliated with it. Generally, it is egalitarian in its approach to both rights and religious obligations, is opposed to intermarriage, and believes in traditional Sabbath observance.

What we know today as **Modern Orthodoxy** was also a 19th-century German development, a practical realization of the vision of the Haskalah, a Jewish version of the Enlightenment pioneered by Moses Mendelssohn (1729-1786) that called on Jews to acquire a secular education, speak the local language, and also to apply rational methods to Torah study. Mendelssohn felt this liberal approach to daily life could be reconciled with continued adherence to Torah, both the written law (the Pentateuch) and the oral law (the Talmud and related rabbinical texts), which were still seen as coming directly from God and as fixed.

Although still far smaller than Reform and Conservative in the United States, Orthodoxy is growing rapidly in numbers everywhere. This is partly because the Orthodox have high birth rates and low rates of intermarriage. A recent poll showed 61 percent of Jewish children in the New York area belonging to Orthodox families (this includes all forms of Orthodoxy, not just Modern Orthodox).

In Israel, and in most other countries, Orthodoxy is generally the default version of Judaism for those who are not secular. But, even among Orthodox, there are variations in observance, as well as in the extent of integration into general society.

Haredi (also called ultra-Orthodox) Judaism rejects the possibility of such integration, and its adherents, especially in Israel, wear distinctive dress and live in segregated neighborhoods, something almost necessitated by their strict levels of observance. Their ideal, particularly for males, is a life of full-time study, but outside of Israel most Haredi men also work. Approximately half of Orthodox Jews are Hasidic Jews. Hasidim is differentiated from other Orthodox Jews by their devotion to a dynastic leader, Rebbe, their distinctive clothing and a greater than average study of the inner aspects of Torah. The largest group is headquartered in Brooklyn, NY.

The statistics regarding synagogue membership, particularly in the U.S., only tell a small part of the story. What is clear is that Orthodoxy has found the most reliable formula for passing Jewish identity on through the generations and that it is on the upswing internationally.

JUDAISM'S THIRTEEN PRINCIPLES OF FAITH

We should note here that Judaism does not have a creed. The universal Jewish emphasis on learning, duty, and obligation is the primary expression of religious life. Deed over creed. But still, what is Judaism and what are its primary beliefs? To answer these questions, we turn to one of Judaism's great teachers, Rabbi Moses ben Maimon, also known as Maimonides or Rambam. He was born in Spain in 1135. In 1159 or 1160, his family moved to North

Africa to escape religious persecution at the hands of a zealous Muslim movement. When he grew up, Rambam became a highly regarded physician. In fact, he was the personal physician of Saladin, the great Muslim leader. But Rambam was not just a man of science, Maimonides was one of the giants of Jewish thought. One of Rambam's great works was his Thirteen Principles of Faith which summarizes the essence of traditional or Orthodox Jewish belief.

Principle 1: *"I firmly believe with complete faith that God exists and that he alone created, creates and will create all things."*
It is a given that God exists. No proof of this fact is necessary. Not only does God exist, but he alone has created everything that has ever existed or will exist. In this regard, the Talmud, a massive compendium of Jewish law and analysis, addresses the reason that God created only Adam on the sixth day of creation, and not both Adam and Eve: so that no one could later say that although God created Adam, perhaps another God created Eve.

But it is not enough to say that God exists and that he alone created the universe. We must also recognize that God is not a passive God. It is only through God's continued involvement in the universe that it continues. Should God will it, the universe would shrivel to nothingness, as it existed before the "big-bang." And if that ever happens, if all the solar systems in all the universe come to an end, God will nevertheless continue to exist. God existed before anything was created and he will exist after everything ends. Time is utterly meaningless as applied to the creator.

Principle 2: *"I firmly believe with complete faith that God is unique and is One."*
The Shema (Deuteronomy 6:4-9) is the centerpiece of the daily morning and evening prayer services and is considered by some

to be the most essential prayer in all of Judaism. An affirmation of God's singularity and kingship, its daily recitation is regarded by traditionally observant Jews as a biblical commandment.

The Shema is recited at the climactic moment of the final prayer of Yom Kippur, the holiest day of the year, and traditionally as the last words before death. Traditionally, it is recited with the hand placed over the eyes.

Judaism was the first monotheistic religion. While other civilizations worshipped many Gods, Jews worshipped the one God. *"Hear, O Israel: The Lord our GOD, the Lord is one. You shall love the Lord your GOD with all your heart, and with all your soul, and with all your might. And these words that I command you today shall be on your heart. You shall teach them diligently to your children and shall talk of them when you sit in your house, and when you walk by the way, and when you lie down, and when you rise. You shall bind them as a sign on your hand, and they shall be as frontlets between your eyes. You shall write them on the doorposts of your house and on your gates." (Deuteronomy 6:4-9)*

The Shema prayer was so influential and important that Jesus used it as His answer to the "greatest commandment" question in Mark 12:28–30:

"And one of the scribes came up and heard them disputing with one another, and seeing that he answered them well, asked him, "Which commandment is the most important of all?" Jesus answered, *"The most important is, 'Hear, O Israel: The Lord our God, the Lord is one. And you shall love the Lord your God with all your heart and with all your soul and with all your might.' The second is this: 'You shall love your neighbor as yourself.' There is no other commandment greater than these."*

Principle 3: *"I firmly believe with complete faith that God is not physical and has no physical characteristics whatsoever."*
Judaism believes that God is formless and incorporeal. He never has had and never will have any bodily form. The basis for this belief is the Bible's account of the Revelation on Mount Sinai when God spoke the words of the Ten Commandments to the Israelites, who heard but did not see the Almighty.

*"**You saw no form of any kind the day the LORD** spoke to you at Horeb **out of the fire. Therefore watch yourselves very carefully, so that you do not become corrupt and make for yourselves an idol, an image of any shape, whether formed like a man or a woman, or like any animal on earth or any bird that flies in the air, or like any creature that moves along the ground or any fish in the waters below. And when you look up to the sky and see the sun, the moon and the stars—all the heavenly array—do not be enticed into bowing down to them and worshiping things the LORD** your **God has apportioned to all the nations under heaven. But as for you, the LORD** took you and brought you out of the iron-smelting furnace, out of Egypt, to be the people of his inheritance **as you now are."** (Deuteronomy. 4:15-20)*

While the Hebrew Scriptures bestow human attributes on God—"eyes of the Lord" or "hand of God"—this is done only because we need assistance in conceiving of the One who is formless incorporeal and inconceivable.

Principle 4: *"I firmly believe with complete faith that God is the first and the last."*
As stated earlier, time is meaningless as applied to God. He is eternal and will continue to exist after everything ceases. Isaiah 44:6 says *"This is what the Lord says—Israel's King and Redeemer, the Lord Almighty: I am the first and I am the last; apart from me there is no God."*

Principle 5: *"I firmly believe with complete faith that it is proper to pray to God and only God and that no one else is to be the recipient of our prayers."*

Jews are prohibited from directing prayers to anyone but God. Pr*ayers devoted to idols, ancestors, or even angels are absolutely and totally forbidden. Moreover, no intermediary is needed in praying to God* since Jews are to pray to God directly. The first of the Ten Commandments states, I am the Lord *your* God, meaning that God is personal to all who believe in him. Consequently, when we pray to God, we can have a relationship that is both direct and intimate.

Principle 6: *"I firmly believe with complete faith that the words of the prophets are true."*

Throughout history, God has communicated with humankind through the prophets, and all the prophecy stated in Scripture is absolutely true. But who are the prophets in the Hebrew Scriptures? There are many. Abraham was a prophet. Moses was too, as were his siblings, Aaron and Miriam. Other prophets included Elijah, Elisha, Ezra, Nehemiah, Isaiah, Jeremiah, Ezekiel, Daniel, Hosea, Joel, Amos, Obadiah, Jonah, Micah, Nahum, Habakkuk, Zephaniah, Haggai, Zechariah, and Malachi. All their teachings and writings are absolutely correct.

While modern Biblical scholarship (which would include the Reform and the Conservative movements) will often take issue with this last point. To the Orthodox Jew, faith in the authenticity of the words of the prophets is fundamental to being Jewish.

Principle 7: *"I firmly believe with complete faith that the prophecy of Moses was the greatest of prophets, of those who preceded him and those who followed him."*

Moses was the greatest prophet because he had a special relationship with God: He was able to communicate with God whenever Moses chose to. This was quite unusual because God spoke to all the other prophets only when God chose to. The Bible tells us that God spoke to Moses "face to face, as one speaks to a friend." Furthermore, Moses was the only one to whom God gave his *Torah*.

Principle 8: *"I firmly believe with complete faith that God himself revealed the Torah to Moses and the Torah that was revealed to Moses is identical to the one we now possess."*
The first five books of the Bible (Genesis, Exodus, Leviticus, Numbers, and Deuteronomy) are often called the Pentateuch, which is Greek for "five books." In Hebrew, these five books are called the *Torah*. *Torah* is often interpreted to mean "Law," but it actually means "instruction." The *Torah* according to traditional belief, was authored by God himself, who dictated it to Moses.

As we shall learn the *Torah* is the cornerstone of Judaism because it is in the *Torah* where we find God's commandments, which are more than ten.

Principle 9: *"I firmly believe with complete faith that God will never change the Torah nor will he ever give another Torah."*
Judaism, like Christianity, believes that God is perfect. Therefore, God could only give a perfect Torah. It is written, *"The law of the Lord is perfect."* A perfect God gave a perfect Torah and it is impossible to improve upon that which is perfect. As the Torah itself says, **"You must neither add anything to what I command you, nor take away anything from it, but keep the commandments of the Lord your God with which I am charging you." (Deuteronomy 4:2-4)**

Principle 10: *"I firmly believe with complete faith that God is omniscient."*

God knows all. The omniscience of God is the principle that God is all-knowing. He encompasses all knowledge of the universe past, present, and future simultaneously. God's knowledge is timeless.

He knows not only all our deeds; he knows our needs also. Nothing can be hidden from the Creator, who knows us so intimately, that he knows even our private thoughts. God's omniscience ensures us of a personal God. As the first of the Ten Commandments states, ***"I am the Lord your God..."*** God is the God of each of us.

Principle 11: *"I firmly believe with complete faith that God rewards those who keep his commandments and punishes those who transgress is commandments."*

God is not only merciful but just too. As such evildoers must be punished since if they were not, the distinction between good and evil would be inconsequential and meaningless. Thus, there must necessarily be reward and punishment, if not now, then in The World to Come.

Judaism has traditionally taught that our reward or punishment is determined by whether we keep gods commandments. As the Torah makes clear in Deuteronomy 30:15-17, ***"See, I set before you today life and prosperity, death and destruction. For I command you today to love the LORD*** your ***God, to walk in obedience to him, and to keep his commands, decrees, and laws; then you will live and increase, and the LORD*** your ***God will bless you in the land you are entering to possess.***

But if your heart turns away and you are not obedient, and if you are drawn away to bow down to other Gods and worship them, I declare to you this day that you will certainly be destroyed.

You will not live long in the land you are crossing the Jordan to enter and possess."

The laws that are referred to here are not just the Ten Commandments. As we shall see later in our study of the laws, there are 613 commandments that bind the Jewish people.

Principle 12: *"I firmly believe with complete faith that the Messiah will come, and though he may tarry, daily is his coming awaited."*
In Jewish eschatology, the Messiah is a future Jewish king from the Davidic line, who is expected to be anointed with holy anointing oil and rule the Jewish people during the Messianic Age and The World to Come. Belief in the future advent of the Messiah is one of the fundamental requisites of the Jewish faith.

For Christians, of course, the Messiah has already come in the person of Jesus. A common question is: If Jews believe in the Messiah, why do they not believe that Jesus is the Messiah? This is an important question and one which must be answered for Christians to have a good grasp of Judaism. The Messiah is the person who will lead humankind into a Golden Age, a time when war, famine, disease, and pestilence will no longer exist. After Jesus' death, the world continued to suffer from these tribulations. Therefore, whoever Jesus was, he could not have been the Messiah.

We will explore this in-depth in the next few pages.

Principle 13: *"I firmly believe with complete faith that there will be a physical resurrection of the dead at a time when it pleases the Creator."*
Judaism, like Christianity, subscribes to the belief in an afterlife of the soul. But in addition to the belief that the soul endures after the body ends, there will also be a bodily resurrection of the dead when the Messianic Age unfolds.

JUDAISM AND CHRISTIANITY—COMMONALITIES AND DIFFERENCES

Commonalities

By focusing on what we share, we can sharpen our appreciation for the ways in which the two traditions have taken the basic truths revealed by God and transformed them into two separate living faiths.

God—Our most important similarity is our deity. We worship the same God, who is also worshipped by the world's 1.97 billion Muslims. We all worship the God of Abraham, whom we believe to be Creator, Revealer, and Redeemer. We believe that this God has given us through our sacred texts, a combination of inspiration, instruction, and commandments that teach us what He wants of us. Our traditions teach us that this God is transcendent but also omnipresent, infinite, eternal, unchanging, omnipotent, creative, omniscient, merciful, compassionate, holy, sovereign, good, and just (to name but a few adjectives throughout our scripture). We see ourselves in a relationship with God who has created us not just to serve Him but to care for his creation. We believe that this relationship, or covenant, has obligations on both sides.

That we hold God to be a God of justice is a critical point, we do not see God the way the Greeks saw their gods, as often playful characters perpetrating tricks and schemes on helpless humans who would turn to bribery to influence them. That God is just, moves Abraham to challenge Him to live up to His own standards regarding the destruction of Sodom and Gomorrah. ***"Shall not the Judge of all the earth deal justly?"*** Abraham asks in Genesis 18:25. When we ask, "where was God at Auschwitz" or why were so many killed in this earthquake?" or "why was my innocent child taken from me" and other questions like this, we make the implicit assumption that God is a just and good God. If this were not so, we would have no basis upon which to question God's actions in the world.

We also hold that God is a God of mercy. Both of our traditions emphasize that God's desire is not to punish the sinner but that the sinner turn from sin and repent. Since mercy is considered to be especially characteristic of the Christian concept of Jesus, that he is ever-forgiving and ever-compassionate and ever-loving, some Christians conclude that the justice-seeking aspect of God must reside in the "Father" element of the Trinity. Since many associate this element with the "God of the Old Testament Jews," they mistakenly conclude that the Jewish view of God is of a God who is primarily concerned with vengeance and punishment. This is not the Jewish view of God, as can be seen in the way *The Gates of Repentance,* the High Holy Day prayer book, addresses God: ***"This is Your glory: You are slow to anger, ready to forgive. Lord, it is not the death of sinners You seek, but that they should turn from their ways and live. Until the last day, You wait for them, welcoming them as soon as they turn to You."***

Scripture—Once again, this simple point needs to be underlined. We share a common, sacred text, which Jews call the *Tanakh* and Christians call the Old Testament. Christianity's retaining the Hebrew Bible is the result of a conscious choice by the early church fathers in the second century.

Our common scriptures give us the basis for improved dialogue and understanding. When we gather together in prayer, we may have the pleasure of praying from the same texts. That we each derive separate lessons and diverse inspiration from these texts, whether it be from Psalms, Proverbs, the book of Job, or the Ten

Commandments, is a testament to their power and universality.

Although we read the same scriptures in the Hebrew Bible, there a few differences worth mentioning. The Christian order of the books of the Bible is not the same as that found in the Hebrew Bible. The Catholic Bible includes a number of books (the Apocrypha) in its "Old Testament" that are not included in the Hebrew and Protestant Bibles. There is also a special way that a Jew studies text—with the commentaries and analyses of others. It is almost unthinkable that a Jewish study of the Bible would not include the opinions and insights from rabbis and experts of the Talmudic and medieval periods alongside the text. While this approach is shared in Catholic traditions, it certainly differs from the *sola scriptura* (scripture alone) approach that is more typical among Protestants.

Moral Principles—This is a point that isn't stressed enough. Both of our traditions teach what has become known as the ***Golden Rule***. The Jewish version is stated in the negative as ***"What is hateful to you, do not do to your fellow man."*** While there are those who would focus on the different motivations of Jews and Christians in their conduct of ethical behavior—those who would stress that Jews are following specific details of Jewish law while Christians are imitating Jesus. Instead, we should focus on actual practice. The bottom line for a Jew is that good works, acts of lovingkindness, of mercy, of charity, included in what Jews would call ***Mitzvot***, are done in the world.

Hope for a Redeemed World—This is another point that is so obvious that it is easy to overlook. Judaism introduced, and Christianity carried into their fundamentals of the faith, the idea of redemption. Both traditions see the world moving from historic and present days of trials and hardships to a future world that is better, even perfect. Both traditions believe that history has direction, that we are not intended to live within a repeating cycle of slavery, despair, hunger, war, and disease. And in both traditions, we find religious people hard at work to improve the world even though they may be motivated by different theologies.

Prayer—How we pray has stayed more similar than different over the centuries. Both of our religions turn to communicate—to speak out and to listen—with God through prayer. In both traditions, prayer consists of both formal liturgies spoken in sacred assembly and in the words and meditations of the heart spoken silently or aloud, within a group or alone. We believe that God listens to and answers prayer, even if sometimes the answer is "No."

Both of our traditions open our worship services with candle lighting. But, no better example of similarity in our prayer life if the **Kiddush** recited every Sabbath and festival. A pitcher of sweet wine, the Kiddush cup and two loaves of freshly baked bread (usually braided challah) complete the table preparation. The two

Jesus, at the Last Supper—knowing he would be leaving his disciples introduced an additional component to the age-old Kiddush. On the night in which he gave himself up for us, he took bread, said the blessing, broke the bread, gave it to his disciples, and said: *"Take, eat; this is my body which is given for you. Do this in remembrance of me."* When the supper was over, he took the cup, said the blessing over the wine, gave it to his disciples, and said: *"Drink from this, all of you; this is my blood of the new covenant, poured out for you and for many for the forgiveness of sins. Do this, as often as you drink it, in remembrance of me."*

loaves of bread remind us of the double portion of manna collected on the day before the Sabbath when our ancestors journeyed in the desert. Just before sundown, the father/leader fills the Kiddush cup with wine and recites a prayer of blessing that has been recited since ancient times: *"Blessed art Thou, O Lord our God, Creator of the fruit of the vine."* The cup of wine is passed to each person. All sip from it.

Next, the father/leader breaks the bread, saying: *"Blessed art Thou, King of the universe, who brings forth bread from the earth."* A piece of bread is given to each person.

An outstanding, unchanged worship component both of our traditions share is the Priestly Benediction. At the end of the Shabbat service, at the end of a marriage ceremony, the father/leader lays his hands on their heads and says: *"May the Lord bless you and keep you. May He make His face to shine upon you and be gracious to you. May the Lord lift up his countenance to you and grant you peace."* This benediction is a favorite of some pastors and is often recited on Sundays.

Differences

Although they began from a common root, Judaism and Christianity parted ways almost two thousand years ago. The split of Christianity and Judaism took place during the first century AD. While the First Jewish–Roman War and the destruction of the Second Temple in 70 AD were main events, the separation was a long-term process, in which the boundaries were not clear cut. As the Acts of the Apostles narrates the expansion of "the Way" in its initial years, it repeatedly highlights conflicts between non-Jesus following Jews and Jesus-following Jews. Let's examine the major areas of Jewish-Christian difference.

✡ **Faith versus Works**—While Judaism certainly does not ignore issues of faith and Christianity does not ignore good works, it is appropriate to say that Judaism emphasizes the role of right actions over right thought. Christianity, on the other hand, stresses faith over deeds. Judaism has no official creed or statement of faith that is used in Bar and Bat Mitzvah or in conversion. Since the vast majority of Jews are Jews by virtue of birth, there is no specific set of beliefs or dogmas to which we must ascribe—Maimonides 13 Principles of Faith notwithstanding. When a rabbi is ordained, he or she takes no vows. The focus in the Jewish tradition is on the performance of *mitzvot—commandments—that God has given us and not simply "good deeds," Jews believe that our obedience to these commandments is the primary desire of God. The Talmud quotes God as saying that **"better that they abandon me but follow my laws."*** The Talmud adds that such observance will bring the Jews back to faith in God. Although the different Jewish movements take different perspectives with respect to the details of Jewish law and *mitzvot*, all would agree that it is our actions in the world, and not our private beliefs, that are of primary importance to God.

This is, of course, to be contrasted with the Christian perspective on faith and works. While Christian scripture acknowledges that ***"faith of itself, if it does not have works, is dead." (James 2:17)*** It stresses that right faith in God and Jesus as savior is primary. Christian history is brimming with Church Councils that have set forth the specific creeds of belief to which adherents must hold. Failure to follow such creeds could result in a charge of heresy. When the belief systems of specific groups of Christians have varied significantly, it has often resulted in another new denomination—adding to the more than 33,000 already in practice. For Christians, the act of faith in Jesus as savior and redeemer is key; salvation depends on God's grace and mercy. In Judaism, the focus is on human adherence to divine commandments—*mitzvot*.

✡ **Meaning of Sin**—The word sin is an example of a term that both Jews and Christians use to mean very different things. Although there are differences by denomination, when Christians use the word *sin*, they refer either to a state of being in sin or to actual sins people commit. The first sense is especially apparent when they speak of "original sin" (the act of Adam and Eve in eating the forbidden fruit in the Garden of Eden) or being in a "state of sin." In this sense, Christians use the word sin first to mean the power of evil over a wounded human nature that needs divine grace to counteract it. Humans have won the full grace of salvation from the effects of original sin by the death of Jesus for all people. Christians receive this saving grace through Baptism. Thereafter, they speak of being in "a state of sin" only for people who do not seek God's forgiveness for their actual sins.

For Jews, sin is not a state of being, but an act in contradiction to God's commandments. One Hebrew word for sin, *chet* (rhymes with late), illustrates this very well. The word is a term from archery meaning "to miss the mark." God gives us a clear target for our behavior, a target that we may miss. People are neither fundamentally good nor evil but have both the inclination to do good and the inclination to do evil battling within them. Sin is an action whose response demands repentance and forgiveness. Perhaps this saying sums this up well: "In Christianity, man sins because he is a sinner; in Judaism, man is a sinner because he sins."

✡ **The Nature of Evil**—Simply put, the disobedience of Adam and Eve in the Garden of Eden is not the problem for Judaism that it is for Christianity and is not considered by Judaism to be "original sin." Jewish daily morning liturgy puts the Jewish perspective very clearly: ***My God, the soul you have given me is pure.*** Our souls are not "stained" by the actions of Adam and Eve. While the Eden story is indeed part of the Torah and the Bible, Jews do not draw the same conclusions and implications from the text. Even in biblical times, there was no Temple sacrifice that addressed original sin nor did any of the prophets refer to it. Thus, if Jews are to understand Christianity's interpretation of the life, death, and resurrection of Jesus as a response and solution to the problem of original sin, it is easy to understand why Jews do not accept this faith. For Jews, Christianity is a solution to a biblical problem that simply does not exist in Judaism.

How does Judaism address the presence of evil in the world? Jews understand that God is responsible for creating both good and evil in the world. As stated in the words of Isaiah 45:7 ***(I am the One) Who forms light and creates darkness; Who makes peace and creates evil; I am the Lord, Maker of all of these.*** God is the author of everything in the world. Traditional Jews upon hearing especially bad news such as the death of a loved one, recite the blessing: ***"Blessed are You, Lord, Our God, King of the universe, the true Judge."*** God has given us free will; people have the freedom to do good or evil, to build hospitals to preserve life or death camps to extinguish it. But when we go astray, we don't blame Adam or Satan; we have no one to blame but ourselves and only we, with God's help, can work toward our own repentance.

✡ **Repentance and Forgiveness**—The Jewish concept of repentance (Hebrew *teshuvah*) is built around the idea of turning or returning. Jews repent for sins by first acknowledging and regretting the sin, next by confessing the sin, and finally by resolving not to repeat the sin in the future. For sins against another person (theft, insult, injury, etc.), one must first restore the damage done to the other and request forgiveness from the other person before divine forgiveness is possible. Jews believe that God cannot forgive sins committed against other people until the sinner has sought and received forgiveness from the victim. Of course, this requirement makes murder an inherently unforgivable sin. This does not mean that the murderer is irreconcilably condemned to eternal punishment. Jews do believe that God will judge our sins against our good deeds with compassion and mercy as well as with justice. Jews do not presume to know how any individual will fare. God alone has the power to forgive sins against God alone (blasphemy, ritual violations, dietary violations, etc.) The most sacred and sober day of the Jewish calendar, *Yom Kippur* (the Day of Atonement), is dedicated to repentance.

For Christians, the forgiveness of sin, whether original sin or specific violations, is an act of divine grace, an undeserved gift from Jesus/God. Christians are assured of God's willingness to forgive sins such as murder that would not be forgivable in Judaism. The key Jewish act of seeking forgiveness of the victim of the sin is not the precondition to divine forgiveness in Christianity that it is in Judaism.

✡ **Redemption and Salvation**—Although Judaism believes in an afterlife, it is a religion that focuses primarily on *this* life. This is particularly apparent with respect to redemption and salvation. Judaism understands these to be primarily aspects of individual and communal life in this world. An individual Jew pursues redemption in this world by performing *mitzvot* in fulfillment of God's commandments. So too does the Jewish people achieve communal redemption and salvation by complying with God's laws. In this way, salvation becomes almost political in nature. Judaism holds that we humans have been given a divine role in God's plan for completing and perfecting the creation of the world. With the coming of the Messianic Age, personal, national, and universal salvation will merge in a world free of war and suffering.

If for Christians, the Messiah has already come, where is salvation? The answer is twofold: First, Jesus will come a second time to fulfill the prophecies concerning world peace and so on. Second, salvation and redemption are to be understood as more personal, relating to one's soul in the world of life after death.

✡ **The Afterlife**—Judaism, while holding that there is certainly life after this one, has little to say about the specifics of that world. Once again, in Judaism, the stress is on how one lives this life rather than on what the next one is all about. Even as God has entrusted us to care for this world, we trust that God will take care of us in the next. Although the *Tanakh* (Hebrew Bible) itself has little to say about the afterlife, rabbinic literature has much comment and speculation but no authoritative descriptions. There are Rabbis who focused on the immortality of the soul and others who believed in reincarnation. Traditional Judaism holds that the physical resurrection of the dead will take place in "the end of days." But this is not a belief shared by the Reform movement. The afterlife is theologically necessary since Jews believe that God is good and just, and it is clear that goodness and sin are not completely rewarded and punished in this world. The Jewish view, however, offers few details with regard to reward and punishment in "The World to Come."

IT'S MORE ABOUT *WHAT* IS THE MESSIAH THAN *WHO* IS THE MESSIAH

As you might guess from the title of this chapter, there is more to the difference between Judaism and Christianity than the single question: "Was Jesus the Jewish Messiah?" This question is more appropriately asked in two parts:

1. Who was—who is—and/or who will be the Messiah?
2. What is the Messiah and, by extension, who and what is God?

The word "Messiah" is an English rendering of the Hebrew word *Mashiach*, which means "anointed." It usually refers to a person initiated into God's service by being anointed with oil, such as a king. (Exodus 29:7, 1-Kings 1:39, 2-Kings 9:3)

When Jews and Christians say the *Messiah*, they say very different things. The concept of the Messiah is very important to Judaism but is by no means central. Jewish teaching captures this well: "If you are planting a tree and you hear that the Messiah has come, first finish planting the tree, then go to greet him."

Very little is written directly about the Messiah in the Hebrew Scriptures. In fact, the title "the Messiah" as a specific personality does not appear at all. While there is not absolute agreement on the details of the Messiah, virtually all Jewish sources would agree on the following points:

1. The Messiah will be fully human and only human. He will be born and die in the natural manner expected of any man. He will be a "son of God" in the same way each and every one of us is a "child of God." He will come from the line of King David.

2. He will be a ruler (probably political and possibly military in the model of King David) and an agent of God who will restore the sovereignty of the Jewish people and usher in the Messianic Age, gathering the Jewish people from exile back to the holy land. (Isiah 27:12-13 and Isaiah 11:12).

3. The Messianic Age will be a time of peace among all peoples ***"they shall beat their swords into plowshares and their spears into pruning hooks," (Isaiah 2:4)*** and even among animals ***"The wolf shall dwell with the***

lamb (Isaiah 11:6) It will be a time when the entire world accepts the one God, *"the earth shall be full of the knowledge of the Lord," (Isaiah 11:9)*

4. The Messiah will not be God. Only God is God and *"God is One" (Deuteronomy 6:4)* For Jews, the concept of God becoming human or taking on human form is foreign. There is no concept of anything resembling the Trinity of Christianity.

5. The Messiah will not be involved in the redemption of sin any more than any human Jewish leader, certainly not by his sacrifice. Only God is described as "Redeemer" in Judaism. Specifically, the Messiah will not come to redeem original sin since Judaism does not believe in original sin. For Jews, the salvation of the world does not depend on the Messiah but upon people doing the will of God as expressed in God's commandments.

Reform Jews have for the most part drawn away from the idea of an individual Messiah. They hold that the goal of Judaism (and of humanity) is to usher in a "Messianic Age" in which the prophecies concerning peace and redemption will take place. Even in traditional sources, there is great disagreement as to what the Messiah will actually do. The ideas range from the mystical, granting him fantastic powers in the tradition of biblical prophets, to the beautiful idea that the Messiah will come one day after he is no longer needed—after we humans have solved the world's problems ourselves. But nowhere is it suggested that the Messiah is other than human.

In the 16-volume Encyclopedia Judaica, the singular article on Messiah covers 10 pages. Compare this with a 25-page article on Marriage and a 40-page article on Moses.

The Messianic Prophecies in the Hebrew Scriptures—One of the central themes of biblical prophecy is the promise of a future age of perfection characterized by universal peace and recognition of God. (Is.2:1-4, 32:15-18, 60:15-18; Zephaniah 3:9; Hosea 2:20-22; Amos 9:13-15; Micah 4:1-4; Zechariah 8:23,14:9; Jer.31:33-34) Specifically, the Bible says he will:

✡   Build the Third Temple (Ezekiel 37:26-28).

✡   Gather all Jews back to the Land of Israel (Isaiah. 43:5-6).

✡   Usher in an era of world peace, and end all hatred, oppression, suffering, and disease.

✡   Spread universal knowledge of the God of Israel, which will unite humanity as one. As it says: ***"God will be King over all the world—on that day, God will be One and His Name will be One" (Zechariah 14:9).***

If an individual fails to fulfill even one of these conditions, then he cannot be the Messiah. Because no one has ever fulfilled the Bible's description of this future King, Jews still await the coming of the Messiah. Christians counter that Jesus will fulfill these when he returns. In the *Tanakh,* no concept of a second coming exists.

ANTISEMITISM

One cannot fully understand Jews and Judaism without understanding antisemitism, that unique form of hatred that Jews have experienced for more than 2500 years. Virtually every country that has had a significant Jewish community (with the important exception of the Americas) has expelled its Jews at some time during its history. Ask your Jewish friends how they or their ancestors came to America and you will have your own glimpse of how antisemitism changed personal histories.

We will explore some of the historical, theological, and psychological reasons for Jew-hatred. It is one thing to explore the history of hate and we will seek to understand this painful subject. And yet it is beyond comprehension that ordinary Germans, raised by their parents to be good and honorable members of society, volunteered for duty that included burning babies alive.

Talk to five people and you will get ten or more explanations for antisemitism. They will tell you Jews have been hated because they are rich, powerful, stubborn, and snobbish (although poor, weak, cooperative, and friendly Jews have not escaped) You might be told that Jews have been the target of racism (although there are Jews of every race). You might hear that Jews have been used as scapegoats, or even that Jews are guilty of having murdered God (some two-thousand years ago). If you read the article on antisemitism in *Encyclopaedia Judaica*, you will find a lengthy discussion (seventy-four pages with illustrations—and this does not include the seventy-eight-page article on the Holocaust itself). But why? Why?

It is only in the last century that we find antisemitism so puzzling. Before this, Jews have always understood Jew-hatred as a consequence of their Judaism. Antisemitism is a response to Jewish beliefs, teachings, and peoplehood. This explains the fact that, with the single exception of the Nazi genocide, in every age Jews could escape persecution by simply joining the majority culture and forsaking their Jewishness.

Judaism rests on three main elements: God—Jewish faith and belief, Torah—Jewish law and custom, and Israel—Jewish peoplehood. Let's look at the ways in which antisemitism is a response to each of these central Jewish elements.

God—It may sound strange to think of it in these terms, but one could argue that Jews were the first religiously intolerant people.

Before Judaism, pagans seem to have tolerated the worship of other gods. In prebiblical and biblical times, if you visited another land, you would worship the gods of that land alongside or instead of your own. Judaism, on the other hand, had the *chutzpah* to say that there is only *one* God, *our* God (and invisible at that!) and that all other gods were false.

Later, Christians opposed Jews and Judaism for their refusal to accept Jesus as Messiah and God. Muslims could not forgive Jews for refusing to accept Muhammad's prophecy and revelation as true. Nazis and Communists could not tolerate the Jewish idea that there is only one source of ethics and values, which was not the Führer, not the Party, not even the popular vote of the people. The idea that Jews have been chosen by God for a particular mission, an idea that is historically central to Judaism, has led to antisemitism as well.

Torah or Jewish Law—There are several elements of Jewish law that have resulted in antisemitism. The Jewish dietary laws make it difficult, if not impossible, for religiously observant Jews to eat with non-Jews. Similarly, observance of the Sabbath has served to keep the Jews separate from the larger world in both ancient and modern times. However, in requiring that Jews live and proclaim Jewish teachings in this world, Jewish law denies Jews the option of living like the Amish of Pennsylvania in their own world, maintaining only a minimum necessary contact with the larger society. Furthermore, the fact that Jews continued to live by Jewish law was a public demonstration of their denial of Christianity and Islam and their teachings. In addition, Jewish requirements regarding education, study, and learning meant that large numbers of Jews were literate and often successful. Observance of Jewish traditions regarding family, community, charity, and abhorrence of violence have also served to make, many non-Jews resentful of their "different-ness". Jews had to do more than simply cling to a different set of beliefs, they had to translate these beliefs into the way they live in an often-hostile world.

Israel or Jewish Peoplehood—Judaism has always defined itself as both a religion and a people or nation. This was true even before 1948 when the *State* of Israel was created. Jews all over the world identify as being a member of the nation or people of Israel. This is one of the most perplexing aspects of Judaism for non-Jews to understand. Zionism is the historical attempt to translate this traditional national element of Judaism into an actual political entity, the State of Israel. At the present time, most antisemitism is focused on this national element of Judaism. Modern Jew-hatred can be disguised as anti-Zionism.

THE HISTORY OF ANTISEMITISM

Although many think that antisemitism is primarily a Christian or Muslim creation, it predates both religions and has been present in those who consider themselves enemies of all religions, namely Nazis and Communists. What follows is the briefest of presentations of a complex and intricate subject.

Antisemitism in the Ancient World—The earliest record of Jew-hatred may be found in the Hebrew Bible itself. The book of Exodus, in describing the birth of Moses, reports that the Egyptian pharaoh decreed the death of all Jewish baby boys as part of a master genocidal plan. The biblical book of Esther tells the story of an attempt to destroy all the Jews of Persia in the fifth century BC. Later on, during Hellenistic and Roman times, Jews were unique in refusing to worship the gods of these dominant cultures and, as a result, subject to hatred. The holiday of Hanukkah celebrates one such episode in which Antiochus Epiphanes attempted to destroy Judaism in 167 BC (despite his tolerance for other religions). Why? Because the Jews refused to accept Antiochus as a god, would not tolerate the desecration of the Holy Temple, and would not allow themselves to be forced to violate their dietary and other religious laws.

Christian Antisemitism—Theologically, understanding Christian antisemitism seems pretty straightforward. Jesus was a Jew whose message was directed to other Jews. Those Jews who didn't become Christian rejected this teaching. As a result., Jews in the first century and in every age since, represent a challenge to the doctrine that the Hebrew Bible clearly and unambiguously points to Jesus as Messiah and God incarnate. Jews read the same Hebrew scripture as do Christians, hold these same words to be holy, and yet come to very different conclusions regarding their meaning.

This situation is exacerbated by several especially troubling elements in the Christian scripture. Such elements are understandable when we consider that the Christian Bible was written during the period of maximum competition between Jews and Christians. For Christianity to be correct, Judaism (or at least the Pharisees) had to be discredited.

Matthew seems to depict the Jews as taking the blame for the crucifixion of Jesus. And not only the Jews of that time, but the Jews of all time will share this guilt. ***"Then answered all the people and said, His blood be on our heads and the heads of our children" (Matthew 27:25).*** Perhaps the early Christians were also trying to minimize the role of Pontius Pilate and Rome in the execution of Jesus so as to court favor with their Roman governors during this critical period. Nonetheless, this verse created the seed for the idea that the Jew, no matter when he lived, is a "Christ-killer." John planted a second recurring theme in this vein, that of Jews' identification of the forces of evil: ***"Ye are of your father the devil, and your will is to do your father's desires" (John 8:44).***

These elements were seized upon and amplified by the early leaders of the church. Listen to the words of Saint John Chrysostom of Antioch, Archbishop of Constantinople, a fourth-century church father **400 years** after the crucifixion:

"Their synagogue or school is to be set on fire…Second, their houses are to be torn down and destroyed in the same way…Third, they are to have all their prayer books and Talmudics taken from them…Fourth, they are to be forbidden henceforth to teach…and praise God, to thank (God), to pray (to God), to teach (of God) among us and ours…Fifth, the Jews are to be deprived totally of walkways and streets… 'Are they not "inveterate murderers, destroyers, men possessed by the devil.'…God hates the Jews and always hated the Jews…It is the duty of the Christians to hate the Jews."

Sadly, examples abound through history, from the Crusades, the Spanish Inquisition, the vehemence of Martin Luther, the Russian pogroms, Hitler's Nazis and the Holocaust, to today's Muslims and the Palestinians.

Nazi Antisemitism—Nazi antisemitism was unique in that it did not offer the Jews the opportunity of conversion or assimilation. It is also unique in the depth and scope of its cruelty and success in murdering Jews. Although the Nazis were racist, racism was just a tool they used to pursue their hatred of the Jews rather than its cause. First and foremost, Jews are not a race. There are Jews of every race.

As incredible as it sounds, there is convincing evidence to support the idea that Hitler pursued the war in order to destroy the Jews rather than the reverse. Most of us know that six million Jews, including more than a million children, were murdered in the Holocaust—about a third of the Jews then alive. Less known is that some 50% of Europe's Jews, including some 80% of the rabbis and full-time students were murdered.

The magnitude of the horror is so distressing, this text will not further explore the Holocaust here.

JEWISH PRAYER AND RITUAL

History of Prayer

Originally, the mitzvah to pray did not include any specific times, nor was there a defined text. Every individual chose his or her own words with which to address the Creator. There was, though, a standard format for prayer: praise for God, followed by asking Him for all one's needs, followed by expressing gratitude for all God has done for us—both collectively and individually.

Following the destruction of the Holy Temple in Jerusalem in 423 BC, the Jews were exiled to Babylon for seventy years. The new generation born in the Diaspora was, for the most part, not fluent in Hebrew—the "Holy Tongue." In fact, many spoke a broken language—a combination of Babylonian, Persian, Greek, and more—preventing them from properly formulating their own prayers.

To address this issue, Ezra the Scribe—together with the Men of the Great Assembly, consisting of 120 prophets and sages—established a standard text for prayer in Hebrew. They also instituted three times for daily prayer: morning, afternoon and night.

The three prayers (a fourth is added after the morning prayers on Shabbat and Jewish holidays) center around the Amidah, a series of nineteen blessings. The morning and evening prayers also incorporate the **Shema** (See page 39), as per the mitzvah to recite it morning and night. Selected Psalms, blessings and prayers complete the picture. By the 2nd century AD, the prayers the way we know it today were formulated.

Communal Prayer

Although one may pray whenever and wherever (if it is an appropriate location for an exchange with the Creator), Jewish tradition encourages communal prayer.

The reason is twofold: a) A venue designated for prayer is one where God is more readily accessible—in fact, a synagogue is considered a miniature replica of the Holy Temple in Jerusalem, where God's presence was prevalent. b) Joining with others gives each individual the power of the community, and their collective deeds and merits.

A Jew needn't invent their own prayers to God. Jews needn't feel that God's response to their worship will be based on how eloquent or poetic his/her words are. The words are the same at each of the day's services, the same on each Sabbath, and on each festival. An observant, knowledgeable Jew can walk into a synagogue anywhere in the world and know where they are in the service. But even an occasional synagogue-goer can pick up a siddur (prayer book) and follow the service in Hebrew or in translation.

With the Exile after the destruction of the Temple, Hebrew ceased to be the only language spoken by the Jews; as its use became more unnatural for Jews in the Diaspora, it became necessary to establish fixed prayers.

When Jesus instructed his disciples to take communion, he did so with two of the several daily blessings:

Before eating bread: *Blessed are You, Adonai our God, Ruler of the Universe who brings forth bread from the earth.*

Before drinking wine: *Blessed are You, Adonai our God, Ruler of the Universe, who creates the fruit of the vine.*

Jewish prayer rituals are designed to reinforce the sense of community. Even if a Jew is unable to pray in Hebrew, they can still say "Amen" after hearing a prayer. To answer "Amen" is to participate in prayer as part of the community of Israel. A Jew prays within an uninterrupted four-thousand-year history of Judaism, of a four-millennium long covenant between God and the Jews, a history that includes some two thousand years of organized and ordered liturgy.

The incredible variety of prayers in the Jewish liturgy suggests the diverse nature of the relationship between God and humanity. In the course of a single service, we may encounter God the Creator, the Redeemer, the Father, the Judge, Rock of Israel, Shield of Abraham, and many others. Each of these personifications of God implies a different relationship between God and the person praying.

Jewish liturgy is the broad category of activities that Jews do in order to invoke God. It includes reciting, chanting, or singing texts; using ritual objects and wearing ritual garments; performing choreographed physical actions and gestures, and reciting blessings. Although Jewish liturgy includes far more than just the texts that are recited, the texts themselves provide a valuable way of understanding what Jewish prayer and worship are all about. Jewish liturgy can be divided up into three main categories: prayers, blessings, and rituals:

- ✡ **Prayers** are recited on a daily basis and have a specific structure to them.
- ✡ **Blessings** are recited on certain occasions, when eating something, or when performing a commandment like lighting candles before the Sabbath.
- ✡ **Rituals** are particular activities, like the Passover seder

Jewish liturgy constantly balances the interplay between using fixed texts and creating a personally meaningful, sincere interaction with God that reflects the intention of the one who prays.

THE EVOLUTION OF PRAYER

Many of the practices that we associate with Jewish worship today date back to the early days of the Second Temple, around 400 BC. Group public prayer in Judaism probably dates back to that period. These early prayer services are believed to have included the *Shema* (See page 39), some Psalms, and Torah readings.

Ezra is believed to have begun the reading of the Torah in a public square in Jerusalem at least four hundred years BC. Regular readings would take place on Mondays and Thursdays, the market days during which men and women would gather to trade and sell. Today, the weekday morning services at which Torah is read still take place on Mondays and Thursdays. Many of the prayers that we still read today date from this period.

The liturgy of this time was almost entirely oral. But the arrival of the Roman imperialists in the second and third century AD led to massive oppression of the Jews, and the rabbis feared for the future of the liturgy. This led to handwritten prayer books for use in worship services.

Although synagogue service was established in something resembling its present form by the time of the destruction of the Second Temple in 70 AD, the first actual prayer book was not compiled until the ninth century. This volume was created by Spanish Jews; the result was a collection of prayers for the entire year and a guide to the regulations that governed them. The volume even included a section outlining the life-cycle events. For the first time in Jewish history, there was a benchmark for worship.

The need for such a worship text was the direct result of the Diaspora, the exile and dispersion of the Jewish community that came in the wake of the destruction of the Second Temple in Jerusalem in 70 AD. Scattered throughout the known world, with no central authority to which they could turn and no central place to which to make pilgrimages, Jewish communities were forced to turn to local scholars and neighborhood synagogues.

The *Siddur*—The *siddur*, or Jewish prayer book, includes the standard texts for the three daily prayer services as well as the additional services for the Sabbath and holidays. Some *siddurim* (plural) also include blessings for various occasions and maybe the weekday Torah readings. The *siddur* has always been a very dynamic text that has grown and changed according to the needs or aesthetics of the various communities in which it was used.

Machzor—The *machzor* is a special prayer book for festivals, usually referring to the High Holiday prayer book is like an incredibly expanded *siddur*, filled with special liturgical poetry and biblical readings appropriate to Rosh Hashanah (the Jewish New Year) and Yom Kippur (the Day of Atonement). The *machzor* contains some of the most memorable texts from Jewish liturgy, including the prayer *Avinu Malkenu* (Our Father, Our King), *Kol Nidrei* (the annulment of vows preceding Yom Kippur), and the confession of sins arranged as alphabetical acrostics (*Ashamnu* and *Al Chet*).

Haggadah—The *Haggadah* is the text that is used during the Passover seder (ritual meal held on the first night of Passover in Israel and most Diaspora liberal communities, and on the first two nights among traditionalist Diaspora Jews). The *Haggadah* includes the choreography and text for a ritual retelling of the story of the Exodus of the Jews from Egypt.

Although there is a traditional text for the Haggadah, new versions come out every year, some of which have new commentaries and new art, and some of which present variations on the traditional text. Some seder hosts create their own Haggadot (plural).

Personal Prayers

Although Judaism wants people to engage God regularly through structured prayer services, it is likely that some of the most sincere and intense prayers have been expressed spontaneously by individuals. Some personal prayers have been recorded, but more frequently these prayers were made during the service in a brief silent prayer time. If a Jew is asked if they pray outside of the synagogue, in their own words. The answer would be "No! We just don't do that."

A Jew prays within an uninterrupted, four-thousand-year history of Judaism, of a four-millennia-long covenant between God and the Jews, a history that includes some two thousand years of organized and ordered liturgy.

The Role of the Rabbi

For the vast majority of modern practicing Jews, Judaism has no hierarchy in worship. The distinction between lay leadership and the rabbinate is much narrower in practice and theory than in most Christian denominations.

About the only thing a rabbi can do in front of a congregation, that can't be done by any ordinary Jew, is signing a marriage license, and that power is not granted by a Jewish body but by the state. That being the case, what exactly does a rabbi do in terms of worship? To some extent, the answer to that question depends on the branch of Judaism to which the congregation belongs and its financial situation.

For example, in a prosperous Conservative synagogue, the congregation may be led by a highly trained cantor, who will lead the entire service. The rabbi may do little more during services than announce page numbers and deliver a sermon. A parallel in larger protestant churches with enough resources, congregants are led by a music minister and one or more associate pastors.

Regardless of what a rabbi knows or does during worship, he or she cannot intercede with God for the congregation. Ultimately every Jew is responsible for his own conversation with God. And what happens in that dialogue is a matter of great concern in Judaism.

BIRTH TO DEATH—THE CYCLE OF LIFE

Birth

God's first commandment to humankind is "Be fruitful and multiply" (Gen 1:28) Judaism has always considered children to be a gift, a blessing from the Creator. Conversely, barrenness was a curse. It should be noted here that the life of the mother takes precedence over that of the unborn infant in all cases. Only when the child's head has emerged from the birth canal is it considered alive; at that point the life of the child takes precedence.

Circumcision

If God did not want men to have foreskins, why did He create them with foreskins in the first place? Many parents of newborn baby boys have pondered this question while deciding whether to circumcise their perfect little son. In fact, the answer can be traced all the way back to the first century AD. God created an incomplete world, leaving human beings to bring it to greater perfection.

In the Torah, God commands Abraham to circumcise himself at age 99. God also specifies that all the generations of Abraham's male descendants must observe this practice, which God calls "the mark of the covenant between Me and you." However, the Torah never indicates *why* circumcision is what marks this very important covenant. Jewish thinkers have advanced their own explanations. Here are a few:

Health & Safety—Philo of Alexandria, a first-century Jewish thinker, first suggested that the foreskin is unclean and can be the cause of disease. In modern medicine, the jury is still out on this issue. Some argue that circumcision is the healthier choice for boys and men, citing a higher risk of cancer in uncircumcised males.

Maimonides, the great medieval Jewish philosopher, rationalist, and physician argued that circumcision weakens, without harming, the male sex organ so that the sexual desires of circumcised men are moderated. The bodily injury caused to the penis, he said, does not interrupt any vital function, but it does counteract excessive lust.

Though Maimonides was a doctor, medicine has changed a lot since the 12th century. Some contemporary medical studies show that circumcision affects sexual pleasure positively, some show it affects sexual pleasure negatively (as Maimonides believed), and others show no difference between circumcised and uncircumcised men. Most medical authorities today are comfortable offering circumcision without concern about significant effects on sexual desire or function.

Jewish Distinctiveness—Maimonides also points out that circumcision prevents those who do not believe in God from claiming to be members of the Jewish religion. Since circumcision is so difficult, no one would undergo it unless he sincerely wanted to belong to the Jewish faith. In a sense, then, circumcision functions like a gatekeeper, keeping Jews "in" and others "out," and contributing to Jewish distinctiveness and survival.

Even Spinoza, the unorthodox 17th-century Dutch Jewish thinker remarked: "Such great importance do I attach to the sign of the Covenant that I am persuaded that it is sufficient by itself to maintain the separate existence of the nation forever." This explanation of circumcision can be compelling for contemporary parents who want to make sure their sons grow up to feel a sense of belonging in the Jewish community. Of course, some would argue that the "distinctiveness" argument is moot in the United States where most of all baby boys are still circumcised.

Submission to God's Will—There is a trend among Jewish thinkers to not advance specific explanations for the commandments, and instead accept that all the commandments contribute to a goal of submitting to God's will. Jewish authorities who accept this line of thinking have argued that the foreskin has no purpose except its removal, an act that symbolizes Jews' willingness to totally obey God. This, they believe, is reason enough to do it.

New parents—for whom life is unpredictable and full of unexpected and unknown experiences—may find it spiritually meaningful to root the beginning of their parenting journey in an age-old ritual that signifies obedience to a higher power.

Bar / Bat Mitzvah

Bar Mitzvah means "son of the commandment." Bat Mitzvah means "daughter of the commandment." According to Jewish law, when Jewish boys become 13 years old, they become accountable for their actions and become a bar mitzvah. A girl becomes a bat mitzvah at the age of 12 according to Orthodox and Conservative Jews, and at the age of 13 according to Reform Jews. This is a momentous event in the life of a Jewish boy or girl and well worthy of celebration. The designated ages are the ones at which a Jew is considered by Jewish law to be able and ready to fulfill the *mitzvot*, the central tenets of the Jewish religion. Not only ready and able but obligated to do so. At this age, one is now a full-fledged recipient of the religious heritage of the Jewish people and a member of the community.

Engagement and Marriage

Jewish engagements can last a week, or they can last several years. Among Orthodox Jews, however, engagements are short; once the decision has been made, and an engagement document signed, there is no reason to delay. Given that Orthodox couples will have no physical contact before the marriage, it also seems the considerate thing to do for the young couple.

The day before the wedding, a traditionally observant bride will visit the mikveh/ritual bath to immerse herself. On the day of the wedding, just before the ceremony itself, the ketubah is signed by two witnesses. This is followed by a legal contract between the parents agreeing that their children will be married. In the days of Jesus, the engagement document was written to be difficult to abrogate if the couple changed their minds. Joseph and Mary's parents may have signed the contract while Jesus' parents were still children.

The Hebrew word for the marriage ceremony means sanctification. Marriage is viewed by Judaism as a sacred act, also an imperative one. In the time of the Temple, the high priest was not permitted to conduct the Yom Kippur rites if he was unmarried. The Talmud states explicitly that one of the duties of a father is to see his son married and to provide enough material support that his daughter will be marriageable. Even God is "married" to the Jewish people. In Hosea 2:21, God says, *I will betroth you unto Me forever.* Similarly, Jews greet the Sabbath as a bride.

Marriage as an institution is as much the creation of God as anything in the Torah. "It is not good for man to be alone," the Creator says of Adam in Genesis 2:18 before creating Eve as his companion. By investing marriage with a Divine origin, Judaism gives it even greater weight and sanctity.

A Jewish wedding begins with the parents of both the bride and groom leading their children to the chuppa (marriage canopy). There is no "giving away" of the bride; she is not the property of her father. The ceremony doesn't just signify the joining of two individuals, but two families.

There is one part of the Jewish wedding ceremony that everyone, even non-Jews are familiar with. After the vows and exchanging of rings, the groom is handed a glass covered in a white cloth; he places it on the ground and steps on it with his right heel, shattering it. The sound of the breaking glass triggers a wave of shouts of Mazel Tov (Good luck!").

In traditional Judaism, marriage is viewed as a contractual bond commanded by God in which a man and a woman come together to create a relationship in which God is directly involved. (Deuteronomy. 24:1) Though procreation is not the sole purpose, a Jewish marriage is traditionally expected to fulfill the commandment to have children. (Genesis 1:28) In this view, marriage is understood to mean that the husband and wife are merging into a single soul, which is why a man is considered "incomplete" if he is not married, as his soul is only one part of a larger whole that remains to be unified.

Abortion

As may be surmised from its attitudes toward birth, Judaism does not accept the Catholic notion that life begins at conception. At the same time, however, even the most politically progressive movements in American Judaism reject the idea of abortion "on demand."

Divorce

Given the sanctity with which it approaches marriage, it is no surprise that Judaism considers divorce a grave step. Divorce has always been possible in Judaism, but it has had a legal character so that it cannot be entered into lightly. It is regarded as a last resort whose invocation is nothing less than tragic.

Conversion to Judaism

Judaism does not actively proselytize, does not seek out converts. However, it wasn't always that way. Abraham opened the flaps of his tent, and welcomed the stranger, telling him of Adonai, the one true God, and urging him to put aside idolatry and polytheism. While he was speaking to the men, his wife Sarah would speak to the women.

Abraham and Sarah provided an example that Jesus and his followers took to heart quite successfully. At the time of his death, Jesus could number 120 among his group. When Christianity was proclaimed the official faith of the Roman Empire, proselytizing by the Jews was forbidden on pain of death. Jews would be allowed to circumcise their own sons, but it would be illegal to circumcise non-Jews.

Traditionally, rabbis have initially tried to discourage a non-Jew who asks to convert. When the rabbi has determined that the convert is sincerely motivated and has achieved a satisfactory level of Jewish knowledge and practice, S/he will go before a rabbinical court which will interview him/her to ascertain their level of understanding and acceptance of the commandments and other facets of the religion. A male convert will undergo circumcision. If he is already circumcised, he undergoes a symbolic pinprick at the place of the circumcision. Finally, both male and female converts undergo immersion in the mikveh. The new convert is given a Hebrew name. The convert is a full-fledged Jew. S/he is welcomed as one who has begun life over again. Any of the privileges, rights, and responsibilities that a Jew by birth has are the same for a "Jew by choice."

Death and Mourning

Life is cherished and preserved, longevity is a blessing, and premature death a tragedy. The prophet Isaiah declares that eventually "God will destroy death forever."

Needless to say, Judaism views the process of dying with great sobriety. A dying person should not be left alone. Judaism has no formal deathbed sacrament and does not demand a final confession. It is a source of merit that a dying Jew's last words be the Shema. (See Page 45)

Jewish law opposes euthanasia or physician-assisted suicide. It is forbidden to manipulate a dying Jew in a manner that would speed up the dying process. On the other hand, it is permissible to remove life support.

When death finally comes, the eyes and mouth are closed. The body is covered with a sheet to maintain its dignity. The corpse is not to be left alone from the moment of death until burial. It is Jewish practice to bury the dead within twenty-four hours of death if possible. Burial may not take place on the Sabbath or the festivals.

One part of the actual burial that some people find disturbing is the practice of having each person present at the graveside, beginning with the immediate family, take a shovel and place three shovelfuls of dirt in the grave.

The mourning process, Shiva, takes its Hebrew name from the length it lasts, seven days. Mirrors will be covered or turned to the wall. As on Yom Kippur, mourners do not wear leather shoes. In Orthodox families, mourners are forbidden to shave, bathe, go to work, or study Torah.

This is a time when a community comes together to help a family remember their loved one, bringing food so that the mourners needn't be distracted by mundane tasks like cooking. Shiva is suspended for the Sabbath. Shiva ends on the morning of the seventh day after death.

Kaddish

Kaddish is a prayer that should be familiar to even nonobservant Jews because it is the payer for mourners. The prayer is a hymn of praise to Adonai, calling for the establishment of God's sovereignty. The recitation of the Mourner's Kaddish allows the bereaved to lead the community in praising God. Being able to restore one's faith in God after the experience of losing a loved one is an essential part of the grieving process for a person of faith; saying Kaddish is a moving part of that process. At the same time, it is a way of honoring the deceased by praising Adonai in their name.

The Afterlife

Jewish thought does not reject the idea of a life after death. The Torah is rather vague on the specifics of such an existence. The

Bible does refer to Sheol as the place to which the dead go, but it is unclear whether this involves more than mere burial.

Belief in the resurrection of the dead, a key element in traditionally observant Judaism's vision of the Messianic age, dates from the period of the Pharisees. It is in the Hellenistic period that the term Olam Ha-Bah (the World to Come) first gained currency. The Mishnah explicitly states that corporeal resurrection will be a part of the World to Come.

Most observant Jews believe in the eventual resurrection in some form, although the idea of the immortality of the soul is not dependent on bodily resurrection in Jewish thought.

C.S. Lewis once said that what you believe about the afterlife changes everything about how you live your life. If you believe there's an afterlife, then you're willing to take risks. You don't believe this is the end. When you face death, the death of a family member, somebody you care about, you know it's just goodbye for now. So, how you grieve is different.

Protestants believe in the afterlife in heaven because Jesus talked about it. Christians think He was right about who He was and what He said, and so, because we believe in Him, we believe in what He said. Jesus demonstrated there was an afterlife by His resurrection. And so, if you believe in His resurrection. He said, **'Because I live, you shall live also.'** We believe the testimony of those who saw Jesus risen from the grave. And we believe that in His resurrection, He was addressing this fundamental dimension of our human existence, our fear of death, the fact that all of us are going to face death someday, and in Jesus' resurrection, he was saying, 'You don't have to be afraid because this is not the end.'

JEWISH LAW

Judaism is both a religion and a legal system comprising three categories of laws: criminal, civil, and religious. The laws of Judaism are more numerous than those found in the Decalogue, the Ten Commandments.

At the heart of Jewish law is from Leviticus 19, in which God says to the people Israel, "You shall be holy for I, Adonai your God, am holy." If one is made in the image of the Almighty, it follows that one should behave in the manner of the Holy One, to do honor to that image, and to render thanks unto the One who made us. That is a tall order to imitate God. Judaism gives a pretty complete series of answers to the basic question of what it would mean to live one's life in God's way. The answer is found in the Torah itself and is elaborated in thousands of pages of rabbinical writings: There are 613 ways to imitate God.

The Fulfillment of the Law

Jesus said, "Do not think that I have come to abolish the Law or he Prophets; I have not come to abolish them but to fulfill them. For truly I tell you, until heaven and earth disappear, not the smallest letter, not the least stroke of a pen, will by any means disappear from the Law until everything is accomplished. So, whoever disobeys the least of these commands and teaches others to do so will be called the least in the Kingdom of Heaven. But whoever obeys them and so teaches will be called great in the Kingdom of Heaven." (Matthew 5:17-19)

The Need for Laws in the New Nation of Israel

With the Exodus from Egypt and the subsequent Revelation on Mount Sinai, The Jewish people were poised to take possession of the land which God had given them when he entered into his covenant with Abraham. The Jewish people had thus become a nation. But what were to be the laws for the new nation? Certainly, the Ten Commandments were to form an integral part of the jurisprudence of the Jewish people. But as with any nation, to regulate the many aspects of life, numerous laws would be necessary.

The Mosaic Covenant is a treaty God made with the Jews, the nation of Israel. What was the point of the book of Deuteronomy? Deuteronomy is the second time the law is given. It is first given in Exodus when Moses is at Mount Sinai. Before Moses dies, and after 40 years of wandering in the desert, the first generation dies away. The new generation, under Joshua, takes the land. Moses gives that same law a second time in Deuteronomy to the new generation that is now meant to take the land and live according to this law as a nation. The important thing is that this is an agreement that God made with Israel. It is not an agreement God made with anyone else.

There are 613 commandments given by God in the Torah—365 negative commandments and 248 positive commandments. (See Appendix)

Positive commandments consist of duties to be performed such as wearing tefillin or putting up a mezuzah, celebrating the festivals, giving to the poor. Negative commandments are prohibitions. Do not place a stumbling block before the blind. You shall not eat unclean animals. Have no other gods before Adonai.

Many of the commandments cannot be observed now, following the destruction of the Second Temple, although they still retain religious significance. According to one standard reckoning, there are 77 positive and 194 negative commandments that can be observed today, of which there are 26 commands that apply only within the Land of Israel.

The New Testament word for Law is Nomos. This is where we get the word Theonomic [Theo = God—Nomos = Law]. The New Testament is just as much God's Law as the Torah. Since God is the lawgiver, and His word is His law, then it follows that every Word which proceeds from His mouth is His law. The New Testament is as much God's law as the Old. The two are One harmonious union. Furthermore, the New Testament explains the Old.

THE 613 LAWS OF THE OLD TESTAMENT CALLED THE MITZVOT

A simplified listing (see Appendix) of the laws of God as they were understood by the Old Testament Hebrews, and the Hebrew people of the present day. The Hebrew word for "LAW" is Torah. In its most limited definition, it refers to the Pentateuch. Yet, the word, Torah, is used to speak of the entire Old Testament as well. Torah basically means "to teach or to instruct". It infers to either human instruction or Divine instruction. Through the law, God shows His interest in all aspects of man's life. Motivated by love, God instructs His people in the ways of wisdom and knowledge. Since God's law is given for our good, its regulations, both negative and positive are for our protection and prosperity. The law is the revealed mind of God. His will is His commandment, and His commandment is His law. Thus, the law is Divine since it comes from a Divine source. It is also perfect, as God Himself is perfect. God's law supersedes all other laws. It transcends all other law, making it the supreme law of the entire earth. God's law is also comprehensive and universal. It speaks to all areas of life, and to every living soul upon the face of the earth. The law speaks of ceremonial truths, moral truths, and dietary truths. It speaks of man's duty toward God, and man's duty toward his fellow man. The Law addresses, philosophy, psychology, biology, physics, all other sciences, economics, ecology, Theology, culture, politics, military relations, international and domestic relations, family life, church life, business, criminal and civil law, and every other aspect of life thinkable. There is nothing that God's Law fails to address specifically. God regulates all life by His perfect law.

God the Author

Who is the author of the Torah, and therefore, of the laws of Judaism? As stated in the Thirteen Principles of Faith, the Torah is the literal word of God. Each and every word was spoken by God to Moses, who dutifully wrote it down. That work, originally in the Hebrew language, and copies of it were subsequently passed down from generation to generation. Of course, the original, like the tablets of the Ten Commandments, is either lost or remains hidden. But the traditional Jewish view is that the Hebrew-language text that is available now is the exact same text that was given to Moses 3,600 years ago at Sinai.

The Oral Law

In addition to the written Torah, God also gave Moses the Oral Torah to clarify and elucidate the many finer points of the written Torah. In Hebrew, this oral Torah is commonly called the *Mishnah*. The Mishnah itself states: "Moses received the law (written and oral) from God at Sinai and transmitted it to Joshua. Joshua transmitted it to the elders. The elders transmitted it to the prophets. The prophets transmitted it to the men of the Great Assembly."

Although the Mishnah was orally transmitted for many centuries, Rabbi Judah, one of Judaism's great sages, reduced it to writing around the year 200 AD. Why did Rabbi Judah break with tradition and put the Mishnah to writing? By the year 200 AD, the land of Israel had ceased to exist as an independent nation. The Jewish people were largely in exile. Rabbi Judah, concerned that the structure necessary to ensure the proper transmission of the Mishnah might one day cease to exist, penned and edited the Mishnah to preserve it for the Jewish people for all time.

The Mishnah Clarifies the Torah—the Gemara clarifies the Mishnah. From the time of the second century BC until the fifth century AD, the rabbis of Babylon and Jerusalem engaged in the study and debate of the Mishnah. These debates were themselves put to writing as a commentary on the Mishnah. In Hebrew, this commentary is called the Gemara, which means "completion," since the Gemara completes the Mishnah.

The Greatest Commandments

Many Christians (and even the Pharisees in Matthew 22:34-36) ask, "which of the 613 commandments of the Torah are the most important?" This question is significant because nowhere does the Torah itself provide a ranking for the commandments. Many think that the Ten Commandments are the most important. But again, the Torah does not say that the Ten are more important than any of the other 603 commandments. We might think that murder is a more grievous sin than eating pork. Murder carries the death penalty and eating pork only lashes. But observant Jews will no more eat pork than they will murder because both are prohibited by God. Because the Torah is the work of God, devout Jews will obey all of the commandments. So, in a sense, all the commandments are of equal importance.

Who is a Jew?

First, let's clear up a myth. Jews are not a "race". Jews are found in a variety of racial classifications: Caucasian, Asian, and Black. It might be best to describe Jews as a "People". An individual is born into the Jewish people and is a Jew for life irrespective of their beliefs. Furthermore, one can also become a Jew by choice, that is, by converting to Judaism. Obviously, if being a Jew were solely a matter of blood and genes, conversion would not be possible. Once someone converts to Judaism, fellow Jews are forbidden to remind the person of his or her non-Jewish roots; the convert is fully Jewish in the eyes of Jewish law, as if from birth.

Under traditional Jewish law, a person is Jewish if he or she is born to a Jewish mother (who herself either was born to a Jewish mother or became a convert to Judaism before the birth of her child). If a person is born to a non-Jewish mother, the person is not Jewish.

The basis for this rule is found in the Torah. In prohibiting marriages between the children of Israel and the seven nations inhabiting Canaan, the Torah states: ***"Do not intermarry with them, giving your daughters to their sons or taking their daughters for your sons because they will turn your sons away from following Me to serve other gods. Then the anger of the Lord will burn against you, and He will swiftly destroy you...." (Deuteronomy 7:3)***

As to whether a person can be part Jewish—at the risk of redundancy, if the mother is Jewish, the child is Jewish; if the mother is not Jewish, the child is not Jewish. There are no "half-Jews" or "quarter-Jews". Devotion and observance of Jewish law do not have an effect on this simple and yet strict definition of who is a Jew. Conversely, if a Jew disavows God and the Torah or converts to another religion, he or she is still a Jew. Once a Jew, always a Jew.

Each Jew feels attached to every other Jew in the world since we are all part of one people. Thus, when Jews in the former Soviet Union or Ethiopia are in need, Jews around the world will come to their aid. The **Law of Return** of the State of Israel provides that any Jew has automatic citizenship as an Israeli and therefore needs no naturalization process. Jews are a people that transcend borders and races and cultural categorizations. In a sense, the State of Israel is the ultimate melting pot, with Jews of some 130 nations coming together to fulfill the provisions of the covenant.

THE PURITY AND HOLINESS CODE

Regulations concerning purity and holiness are found in many cultures in different parts of the world. The terms 'clean' and 'unclean' did not then refer to cleanliness and getting dirty in the present sense of the words. Rather it was a question of the kind of actions, substances, matters, objects, and places which it was desired to place out of bounds for the community.

In early Judaism attitudes towards the purity and holiness code contained in the Torah or Law of Moses varied: in the Diaspora, Jews were more liberal-minded than in Palestine, among the Pharisees and Essenes stricter than outside these groups. In any case, the purity code seems to have grown in importance as the beginning of the Christian era approached.

According to the Torah, a person became unclean if he or she touched something unclean. If he or she was unclean he or she was not allowed to encounter clean people or objects. In some cases, uncleanness disappeared by itself after a determined period had elapsed. Sometimes, to become clean one was required to offer a sacrifice and/or perform ritual washing. Typical sources of uncleanness were bodily secretions, corpses, unclean animals and wrongly prepared food.

Holiness, too, was based on being untouched. If the holy and unclean came into contact, one or other ceased to exist: the holy became unholy or it destroyed the unclean thing. Therefore, the holy had to be separated from the areas of everyday life that were susceptible to uncleanness to form an area of its own. This might happen in several different ways.

The way of protecting holiness might be a time-limit: feast-days such as the Sabbath and the annual festivals were sanctified by excluding everyday activities such as work. This made it possible to observe rites that demanded holiness at these times.

The boundary might be one of space. The holiest was in the heart of numerous concentric boundaries: Israel is a holy land, the holiest place of which is Jerusalem, the holiest place of which is Mount Zion, the holiest place of which is the Temple, the holiest place of which is the Holy of Holies.

Further, the boundary might be between people. Israel was a holy people, which was distinguished from the Gentiles by the fact that Israel observed the Law of God. The concrete manifestations of this obedience were male circumcision, the dietary rules and the observance of the Sabbath. The holiness of the priests was to be greater than that of the ordinary people. One of the characteristic features of the Pharisees was that they endeavored to observe the purity code of the priests.

In general, purity and holiness codes tend to be reinforced when the identity of the community is threatened. Boundaries remind the members of the community who they are. For the same reason, the purity and holiness code played an important part when Christianity diverged from Judaism. When the principal external identifying features of Judaism were no longer required for membership in the community, Judaism was left behind. Christianity had become an independent movement.

DIETARY LAWS

Kashrut is the body of Jewish law dealing with what foods can and cannot be eaten and how those foods must be prepared. The word "*Kashrut*" comes from the Hebrew meaning fit, proper or correct.

The word "*kosher*," which describes food that meets the standards of *kashrut*, is also often used to describe ritual objects that are made in accordance with Jewish law and are fit for ritual use. Food that is not kosher is referred to as *treif* (literally torn).

Kosher is not a style of cooking and therefore there is no such thing as "kosher-style" food. Any kind of food—Chinese, Mexican, Indian, etc.—can be kosher if it is prepared in accordance with Jewish law. At the same time, traditional Jewish foods like knishes, bagels, blintzes and matzah ball soup can all be *treif* if not prepared in accordance with Jewish law.

Why Do Jews Observe the Laws of Kashrut?

Many modern Jews think that the laws of *kashrut* are simply primitive health regulations that have become obsolete with modern methods of food preparation. There is no question that some of the dietary laws have beneficial health effects. For example, the laws regarding kosher slaughter are so sanitary that kosher butchers and slaughterhouses are often exempted from USDA regulations.

However, health is not the main reason for Jewish dietary laws and in fact, many of the laws of *kashrut* have no known connection with health. To the best of our modern scientific knowledge, there is no reason why camel or rabbit meat (both *treif*) is any less healthy than cow or goat meat. In addition, some of the health benefits derived from *kashrut* were not made obsolete by the refrigerator. For example, there is some evidence that eating meat and dairy together interferes with digestion, and no modern food preparation technique reproduces the health benefit of the kosher law of eating them separately.

The short answer to why Jews observe these laws is because the Torah says so. The Torah does not specify a reason for these laws but for an observant Jew there is no need for a reason—Jews show their belief and obedience to God by following the laws even though they do not know the specific reason.

Torah scholars suggest that kashrut laws are designed as a call to holiness. The ability to distinguish between right and wrong, good and evil, pure and defiled, the sacred and the profane, is very important in Judaism. Imposing rules on what you can and cannot eat ingrains that kind of self-control. In addition, it elevates the simple act of eating into a religious ritual. The Jewish dinner table is often compared to the Temple altar in rabbinic literature.

Is Keeping Kosher Difficult?

Keeping kosher is not particularly difficult in and of itself; what makes keeping kosher difficult is the fact that the rest of the world does not do so.

The basic underlying rules are fairly simple. If you buy your meat at a kosher butcher and buy only kosher certified products at the market, the only thing you need to think about is the separation of meat and dairy.

Keeping kosher only becomes difficult when you try to eat in a non-kosher restaurant or at the home of a person who does not keep kosher. In those situations, your lack of knowledge about your host's ingredients and the food preparation techniques make it very difficult to keep kosher. Some commentators have pointed out, however, that this may well have been part of what G-d had in mind: to make it more difficult for us to socialize with those who do not share our religion.

The Fundamental Rules of Kashrut

Although the details of *kashrut* are extensive, the laws all derive from a few fairly simple, straightforward rules:

1. Certain animals may not be eaten at all. This restriction includes the flesh, organs, eggs, and milk of the forbidden animals.

2. Of the animals that may be eaten, the birds and mammals must be killed in accordance with Jewish law.

3. All blood must be drained from the meat or broiled out of it before it is eaten.

4. Certain parts of permitted animals may not be eaten.

5. Meat (the flesh of birds and mammals) cannot be eaten with dairy. Fish, eggs, fruits, vegetables, and grains can be eaten with either meat or dairy. (According to some views, fish may not be eaten with meat).

6. Utensils that have come into contact with meat, may not be used with dairy, and vice versa. Utensils that have come into contact with non-kosher food, may not be used with kosher food. This applies only where the contact occurred while the food was hot.

7. Grape products made by non-Jews may not be eaten.

THE DETAILS

Animals That Cannot Be Eaten

Of the **"beasts of the earth"** (which basically refers to land mammals, with the exception of swarming rodents, you may eat any animal that has cloven hooves and chews its cud. (Leviticus 11:3; Deuteronomy 14:6.) Any land mammal that does not have both of these qualities is forbidden. The Torah specifies that the camel, the rock badger, the hare, and the pig are not kosher because each lacks one of these two qualifications. Sheep, cattle, goats, and deer are kosher.

Of the things that are in the waters, you may eat anything that has fins and scales. (Leviticus 11:9; Deuteronomy 14:9.) Thus, shellfish such as lobsters, oysters, shrimp, clams and crabs are all forbidden. Fish like tuna, carp, salmon, and herring are all permitted.

For birds, the criteria are less clear. The Torah lists forbidden birds (Leviticus 11:13-19; Deuteronomy. 14:11-18,) but does not specify why these particular birds are forbidden. All of the birds on the list are birds of prey or scavengers, thus the rabbis inferred that this was the basis for the distinction. Other birds are permitted, such as chicken, geese, ducks, and turkeys.

Of the **"winged swarming things"** (winged insects), a few are specifically permitted (Leviticus 11:22), but the Sages are no longer certain which ones they are, so all have been forbidden. Rodents, reptiles, amphibians, and insects (except as mentioned above) are all forbidden. (Leviticus 11:29-30, 42-43.)

As mentioned above, any product derived from these forbidden animals, such as their milk, eggs, fat, or organs, also cannot be eaten. Rennet, an enzyme used to harden cheese, is often obtained from non-kosher animals, thus kosher hard cheese can be difficult to find.

Kosher Slaughter (*Shechitah*)

The mammals and birds that may be eaten must be slaughtered in accordance with Jewish law. (Deuteronomy 12:21). We may not eat animals that died of natural causes (Deuteronomy 14:21) or that were killed by other animals. In addition, the animal must have no disease or flaws in the organs at the time of slaughter. These restrictions do not apply to fish; only to the flocks and herds (Numbers 11:22).

Ritual slaughter is known as *shechitah*, and the person who performs the slaughter is called a *shochet*. The method of slaughter is a quick, deep stroke across the throat with a perfectly sharp blade with no nicks or unevenness. This method is painless, causes unconsciousness within two seconds, and is widely recognized as the most humane method of slaughter possible.

Another advantage of *shechitah* is that it ensures rapid, complete draining of the blood, which is also necessary to render the meat kosher. The *shochet* is not simply a butcher; he must be a pious man, well-trained in Jewish law, particularly as it relates to *kashrut*. In smaller, more remote communities, the rabbi and the *shochet* were often the same person.

Draining of Blood

The Torah prohibits the consumption of blood. (Leviticus 7:26-27; Leviticus 17:10-14.) This is the only dietary law that has a reason specified in the Torah: we do not eat blood because the life of the animal is contained in the blood. This applies only to the blood of birds and mammals, not to fish blood. Thus, it is necessary to remove all blood from the flesh of kosher animals.

The first step in this process occurs at the time of slaughter. As discussed above, *shechitah* allows for the rapid draining of most of the blood. The remaining blood must be removed, either by broiling or soaking and salting. The liver may only be kashered by the broiling method because it has so much blood in it and such complex blood vessels. This final process must be completed within 72 hours after slaughter, and before the meat is frozen or ground. Most butchers and all frozen food vendors take care of the soaking and salting for you, but you should always check this when you are buying someplace you are unfamiliar with.

An egg that contains a blood spot may not be eaten. This isn't very common, but they are found once in a while. It is a good idea to break an egg into a container and check it before you put it into a heated pan because if you put a blood-stained egg into a heated pan, the pan becomes non-kosher.

Forbidden Fats and Nerves

The sciatic nerve and its adjoining blood vessels may not be eaten.

The process of removing this nerve is time-consuming and not cost-effective, so most American slaughterers simply sell the hindquarters to non-kosher butchers.

A certain kind of fat, which surrounds the vital organs and the liver, may not be eaten. Kosher butchers remove this. Modern scientists have found biochemical differences between this type of fat and the permissible fat around the muscles and under the skin.

Separation of Meat and Dairy

On three separate occasions, the Torah tells us not to "boil a kid in its mother's milk." (Exodus 23:19; Exodus 34:26; Deuteronomy 14:21). The Oral Torah explains that this passage prohibits eating meat and dairy together. The rabbis extended this prohibition to include not eating milk and poultry together. It is, however, permissible to eat fish and dairy together, and it is quite common. It is also permissible to eat dairy and eggs together.

This separation includes not only the foods themselves, but the utensils, pots, and pans with which they are cooked, the plates and flatware from which they are eaten, the dishwashers or dishpans in which they are cleaned, and the towels on which they are dried. A kosher household will have at least two sets of pots, pans, and dishes: one for meat and one for dairy. See Utensils below for more details.

One must wait a significant amount of time between eating meat and dairy. Opinions differ and vary from three to six hours. This is because fatty residues and meat particles tend to cling to the mouth. From dairy to meat, however, one need only rinse one's mouth and eat a neutral solid like bread, unless the dairy product in question is also of a type that tends to stick in the mouth.

The Yiddish words *fleishig* (meat), *milchig* (dairy) and *pareve* (neutral) are commonly used to describe food or utensils that fall into one of those categories. Even the smallest quantity of dairy (or meat) in something renders it entirely dairy (or meat) for purposes of *kashrut*. For example, most kinds of margarine are dairy for kosher purposes, because they contain a small quantity of whey or other dairy products to give it a dairy-like taste. Animal fat is considered meat for purposes of *kashrut*. You should read the ingredients very carefully, even if the product is kosher-certified.

Utensils

Utensils (pots, pans, plates, flatware, etc., etc.) must also be kosher. A utensil picks up the kosher "status" (meat, dairy, *pareve*, or *treif*) of the food that is cooked in it or eaten from it and transmits that status back to the next food that is cooked in it or eaten off of it. Thus, if you cook chicken soup in a saucepan, the pan becomes meat. If you thereafter use the same saucepan to heat up some warm milk, the *fleishig* status of the pan is transmitted to the milk, and the *milchig* status of the milk is transmitted to the pan, making both the pan and the milk a forbidden mixture.

Kosher status can be transmitted from the food to the utensil or from the utensil to the food only in the presence of heat, thus if you are eating cold food in a non-kosher establishment, the condition of the plates is not an issue. Likewise, you could use the same knife to slice cold cuts and cheese, as long as you clean it in between, but this is not really a recommended procedure, because it increases the likelihood of mistakes.

Stovetops and sinks routinely become non-kosher utensils, because they routinely come in contact with both meat and dairy in the presence of heat. It is necessary, therefore, to use dishpans when cleaning dishes (don't soak them directly in the sink) and to use separate spoon rests and trivets when putting things down on the stovetop.

Dishwashers are a *kashrut* problem. If you are going to use a dishwasher in a kosher home, you either need to have separate dish racks or you need to run the dishwasher in between meat and dairy loads.

You should use separate towels and pot-holders for meat and dairy. Routine laundering *kashers* such items, so you can simply launder them between using them for meat and dairy. Certain kinds of utensils can be "*kashered*" if you make a mistake and use it with both meat and dairy.

Grape Products

The restrictions on grape products derive from the laws against using products of idolatry. Wine was commonly used in the rituals of all ancient religions, and wine was routinely sanctified for pagan purposes while it was being processed. For this reason, the use of wines and other grape products made by non-Jews was prohibited. (Whole grapes are not a problem, nor are whole grapes in fruit cocktail).

For the most part, this rule only affects wine and grape juice. This becomes a concern with many fruit drinks or fruit-flavored drinks, which are often sweetened with grape juice. You may also notice that it is virtually impossible to find kosher baking powder because baking powder is made with cream of tartar, a by-product of winemaking.

Kashrut Certification

The task of keeping kosher is greatly simplified by widespread *kashrut* certification. Approximately three-quarters of all prepackaged foods in the United States and Canada, at least, have some kind of kosher certification, and most major brands have reliable Orthodox certification.

The symbols of kashrut certification are all widely-accepted and commonly found on products throughout the United States. It is very easy to spot these marks on food labels, usually near the product name, occasionally near the list of ingredients.

The most controversial certification is the K, a plain letter K found on products asserted to be kosher. All other kosher certification marks are trademarked and cannot be used without the permission of the certifying organization. The certifying organization stands behind the *kashrut* of the product. But you cannot trademark a letter of the alphabet, so any manufacturer can put a K on a product. For example, Jell-O brand gelatin puts a K on its product, even though every reliable Orthodox authority agrees that Jell-O is not kosher.

It is becoming increasingly common for kosher certifying organizations to indicate whether the product is *fleishig, milchig* or *pareve*. If the product is dairy, it will frequently have a D or the word Dairy next to the *kashrut* symbol. If it is meat, the word Meat or an M may appear near the symbol. If it is *pareve*, the word *Pareve* (or *Parev*) may appear near the symbol (Not a P! That means kosher for Passover!). If no such clarification appears, you should read the ingredient list carefully to determine whether the product is meat, dairy or *pareve*.

JEWISH HOLY DAYS AND FESTIVALS

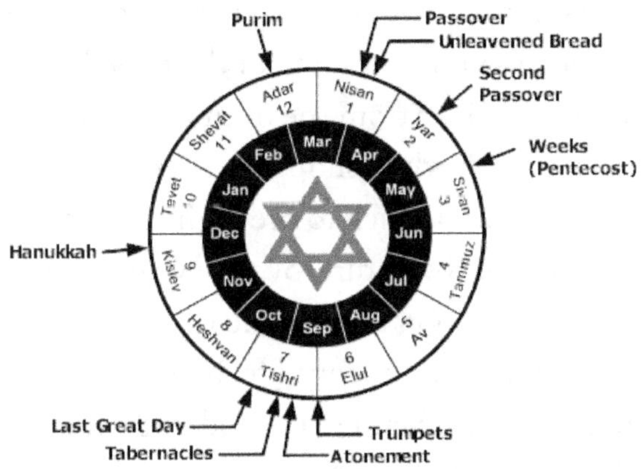

Jewish holidays occur on the same dates every year in the Hebrew calendar, but the dates vary in the Gregorian calendar. The Gregorian is a solar calendar, based on the movement of the earth around the sun. The Hebrew calendar is regulated by the cycles of the moon. A Hebrew month begins with the new moon. Each of the twelve Hebrew months is either 29 or 30 days long, so each year is only 354 days in duration. Obviously, this creates a significant discrepancy between the lunar and solar calendars. In order to make up the difference, the Jewish calendar adds on an additional month in the spring seven times in every nineteen years. The Christian calendar recognizes some holidays—most prominently Easter—as "moveable feasts," but others, like Christmas, for example, are fixed.

The observance of Jewish festivals always begins at sunset the day before the actual date and ends at sunset on the day itself. This is so because the Torah states that God considered the evening as the beginning of the day: *"Evening passed and morning came, that was the first day." (Genesis 1:15)*

Why have the Jews retained this awkward calendrical system? Having a second ritual calendar, one that is markedly different from the one that governs our secular lives, forces us to think in a deliberate manner about the coming of the holy days. It creates a sacred time that is distinct from the ordinary time we experience in our offices, at school, while shopping for dinner. It does so by making us turn our minds back to pre-industrial rhythms, to the rhythms imposed on us by nature, by the cycle of the seasons and the movement of the moon around the earth. We are taken out of the harrowing tempo of modern life, however briefly, to reflect on our covenantal relationship with God and God's creation.

The holidays and the Sabbath are the logical outcomes of this approach to setting aside sacred time. Work is forbidden on the Sabbath and the major festivals. The major festivals consist of the three "Pilgrimage Festivals" and the High Holy Days—The New Year (Rosh Hashanah) and the Day of Atonement (Yom Kippur.) The three Pilgrimage Festivals are Passover (Pesach), Festival of Weeks (Shavuot or Pentecost), and the Festival of *Tabernacles* (Sukkot). When the ancient Israelites lived in the Kingdom of Judah, they would make a pilgrimage to the Temple in Jerusalem, as commanded by the Torah. In Jerusalem, they would participate in festivities and ritual worship in conjunction with the services of the kohanim («priests») at the Temple.

After the destruction of the Second Temple and until the building of the Third Temple, the actual pilgrimages are no longer required of Jews, and no longer take place on a national scale. During synagogue services, the related passages describing the holiday being observed are read aloud from a Torah scroll on the bimah (platform) used at the center of the synagogue services. During the Jewish holidays in modern-day Israel, many Jews living in or near Jerusalem make an effort to attend prayer services at the Western Wall emulating the ancient pilgrimages in some small fashion. Samaritans make pilgrimages to Mount Gerizim three times a year to this day.

SHABBAT—THE SABBATH DAY

It has been said, "More than the Jews have kept the Sabbath, the Sabbath has kept the Jews." The Sabbath is one of the most sacred of the holy days of the calendar even though it comes as often as once each week. Work is forbidden on the Sabbath and the major festivals. The prohibition against working on Shabbat is much stricter than on the Festivals. In the Torah it is written," **By the seventh day God had finished the work he had been doing; so, on the seventh day, he rested from all his work. Then God blessed the seventh day and made it holy because on it he rested from all the work of creating that he had done." (Genesis 2:2-3)**

Shabbat is the only Jewish holiday whose timing does not depend on the calendar at all—seven days are seven days, regardless of the phases of the moon. Like the Creation itself, it is beyond human influence. The Sabbath is the only day of observance mentioned in the Ten Commandments.

The most important, most sacred and joyous day for the Jewish people is the Sabbath. Jews of different religious orientations observe Shabbat in different ways. For example, Orthodox Jews will not drive cars or use public transportation. They will walk to the synagogue. Conservative and Reform Jews generally interpret Sabbath regulations more liberally. But for all Jews, the Sabbath is meant to be a day of spiritual renewal and physical relaxation. Shabbat is a time of turning away from worldly cares and financial concerns.

The Jewish people are encouraged to attend the Sabbath services in the synagogue. The Orthodox and some Conservative congregations maintain a special section for women. But in all other congregations, the people sit wherever they wish. Benches or chairs are provided for the members of the congregation. Kneelers are not needed, as people pray seated or standing during the service. In most synagogues, a box of yarmulkes—skull caps—is placed at the entrance of the sanctuary for males older than thirteen who forgot their own. All males are required to wear a head covering for the service.

Entering the sanctuary, one finds the rabbi and cantor on the bimah. The officers of the congregation and important guests may also be seated on the bimah. The members of the congregation have prayer books to enable them to follow the service and, at times, to participate. Some parts of the service may be recited or sung in Hebrew. The rabbi or cantor indicates when the congregation is to stand or sit and announces the page of the service as it progresses.

The service itself consists of prayers of praise, gratitude, and petition, readings, songs, and short meditations. When it is time for the readings, the rabbi opens the ark and takes out the Torah, giving it to the reader of the day, who brings it to the table or lectern. Blessings are recited before the readings. Following the readings from the Torah, a portion from the Prophets is read. Blessings are again recited, and the Torah is returned to the ark. The rabbi then gives a sermon, usually the teachings from the readings and how they relate to daily life.

Shabbat is a day of **being**, not **doing**. The day's multitude of do's and don'ts are essentially about not making anything, not destroying anything, and simply taking the world as we find it—for one day. The rest of the week, Jews are encouraged to improve the world, better ourselves, and provide for our extended families in whatever roles we find ourselves. But this day: just be. Serve God not in changing the world, but in relaxing into what's already there.

The Sensation of Stopping

In religiously observant homes, Friday afternoon is usually a hectic time. Food to prepare, emails to answer, floors to clean—it can get to be a little much, especially if you've been at work all day. But then, when the candles are lit, a change takes place. Now there's nothing to do. What's done is done, what isn't—isn't, and Shabbat is here.

Tradition has Jews everywhere lighting candles before sunset as a way to mark this important transition. It doesn't matter if it is done *right*, the main thing is to just do it.

Observant Jews use no electricity on Saturdays. Homes are quieter on Shabbat than the rest of the week. No music, no TV, no computers, no phones. There are thirty-nine categories of forbidden work. A few examples: One should not handle money, light a fire, rearrange books on a shelf, cut or tear anything. One day a week is set aside for being with ourselves, a day of detachment from external obligations, a day of freedom from the struggle with our fellow men and the forces of nature.

Shabbat is meant to be a day of peace. The greeting, "Shabbat Shalom" means the Sabbath of Peace. Shabbat is also a time of joy, of good food and wine. It is considered a "mitzvah" (a good deed) to make love with your spouse on the Sabbath.

The concept of joy in the Sabbath is so crucial that any sadness is banished. Fast days are postponed a day if they should fall on Shabbat—except for Yom Kippur. Active mourning is expressly forbidden on the Sabbath. Funerals are put off until Sunday and mourners do not sit Shivah on Shabbat. On Friday, all preparations for the Sabbath must be completed. One should not still be preparing after sundown on Friday.

Shabbat Dinner

The dinner table is covered with a fresh tablecloth. The best dishes and Shabbat candlesticks are set out. The best food is kept for Shabbat. A pitcher of sweet wine, the Kiddush cup and two loaves of freshly baked challah bread complete the table. The two loaves of bread remind us of the double portion of manna collected on the day before the Sabbath when their ancestors journeyed in the desert.

Just before sundown, when all is in readiness and the family has donned their good clothes, the mother lights and blesses the candles, asking God's blessing on her family and home.

בָּרוּךְ אַתָּה יְיָ	Baruch ata Adonoy
אֱלֹהֵינוּ מֶלֶךְ הָעוֹלָם	Eloheinu melech ha-olam
אֲשֶׁר קִדְּשָׁנוּ בְּמִצְוֹתָיו	asher kid'shanu be'mitzvo'sav
וְצִוָּנוּ לְהַדְלִיק נֵר שֶׁל שַׁבָּת.	ve-tzivanu lehadlik ner shel Shabbos.

Blessed are You, God, King of the Universe,
Who made us holy with His commandments
and commanded us to kindle the Shabbat light.

The father then may praise his wife by quoting a passage from the Book of Proverbs or thank her in his own words for all she does for the family. Then he fills the Kiddush cup with wine and recites the **Kiddush,** a prayer of blessing that has been recited since ancient times.

The cup of wine is passed to each person. All sip from it.
Next, the father breaks the bread saying:

בָּרוּךְ אַתָּה יְיָ   Baruch ata Adonoy,

אֱלֹהֵינוּ מֶלֶךְ הָעוֹלָם   Eloheinu melech ha-olam,

הַמּוֹצִיא לֶחֶם מִן הָאָרֶץ.   ha-motzi lechem min ha-aretz.

Blessed are you God, King of the Universe,
Who brings forth bread from the earth.

A piece of bread is given to each person. The father blesses his
children. Laying his hands on their heads, he says:

**"May the Lord bless you and keep you: May the Lord make
his face shine upon you and be gracious unto you. May the Lord
lift up his countenance upon you and give you peace."**

The Sabbath meal is then served. Songs may be sung, or
stories told during and/or after the meal to add to the joyousness
of Shabbat.

The Sabbath day itself is spent in prayer, study, relaxation, and
the companionship of family and friends. The day comes to an
end after sunset on Saturday.

The similarities in the Christian Sabbath observation and rituals to modern Jewish Shabbat rituals cannot be overlooked. Christian Sunday services begin in the sanctuary and include prayers and hymns either standing or sitting. When it is time for the sermon, the Pastor reads first from Scripture, then raises his bible and says, "The word of God for the people of God." The congregation responds, "Thanks be to God"

The Eucharist offers an opportunity to bless the bread and the wine.

Depending on the Pastor's preference, the benediction may be the Priestly Benediction.

Covenant and Commandment

Although there is no mention in the Book of Genesis that human beings should also observe a Sabbath, in the Book of Exodus, God declares that the Israelites should **"Remember the Sabbath day and keep it holy…for in six days the Lord made heaven and earth and sea, and all that is in them, and He rested on the seventh day; therefore the Lord blessed the Sabbath day and hallowed it." (Exodus 20:8, 11).**

Together, these passages give us the profound concept of *imitatio dei*—the imitation of God—in association with Shabbat. We should rest because God rested—and we should "remember" Shabbat and keep it holy. We also implicitly learn that even God needs a break. And if God, the creator of the universe, needed to rest (and sanctified that rest), how much more do we human beings need a weekly opportunity to cease from all productive activities from "creating."

In the Torah God says, **"Remember that you were a slave in the land of Egypt and the Lord your God freed you from there with**

a mighty hand and an outstretched arm; therefore the Lord your God has commanded you to observe Shabbat" (Deuteronomy 5:15) This explanation touches on two momentous motivations for observing Shabbat. The first is the covenant between God and the Jewish people: God redeemed the Israelites from slavery, and the Israelites must observe God's commandments. The second motivation suggested by these phrases is one of deep empathy with our enslaved ancestors. Because our forebears, who were slaves, were unable to enjoy a day of rest, we should observe Shabbat as a demonstration of our own redeemed status—and perhaps, with a consciousness about those who are still enslaved.

Jesus and his Jewish followers participated in the Jewish feasts and joined their kin in synagogue on Shabbat. Jesus wasn't abolishing the Sabbath—he was asking his followers to engage more deeply in the meaning of the Sabbath as a time to celebrate our Creator. Jesus also wanted us to connect Him with the hope the Jewish people had carried for a Messiah who would come to usher in the new creation. He told his followers that he'd come to fulfill the Law, that he was Lord of the Sabbath.

As it was Yeshua's "custom" to enter ***the synagogue on the Sabbath" (Luke 4:16)***, so his followers continued living as pious Jews following the example of their Master.

As the church disconnected from her Hebrew roots, Jewish Sabbath language was overlaid on to these worship gatherings. In 321 AD, Constantine codified this practice with a decree that Sunday would be a day of rest across his empire. The first day of the week had effectively come to be the Christian Sabbath.

THE HIGH HOLY DAYS

The Jewish High Holy Days, also known as The Days of Awe, comprise the holidays of Rosh Hashanah and Yom Kippur and encompass the ten days from the beginning of Rosh Hashanah through the end of Yom Kippur.

The High Holy Days are an important period of introspection, of clarifying life's goals, and of coming closer to God. This period prepares us for the day we stand before the almighty and ask him for another year.

Historically, this month has great significance, because it was on the first day of Elul that Moses—following the sin of the Golden Calf—ascended Mount Sinai to receive a new, second set of stone tablets. Forty days later—on Yom Kippur Moses returned to the people with tablets in hand, signaling a repair of the breach between the Jewish people and God.

Rosh Hashanah

It is generally referred to as the Jewish New Year. Rosh Hashanah literally translates as "Head of the year." It is observed for two days usually in late September. In the Hebrew calendar, it is always the first and second days of the month of Tishrei.

In Jewish tradition, Rosh Hashanah marks the anniversary of the creation of the world as described in the Torah. Sundown on September 29th of 2019 will mark the Hebrew year of 5780.

Although it is seen as a festival, Rosh Hashanah is also regarded as an important and solemn occasion. In Jewish thought, it is seen as being the time when all the people of the world—Jewish and non-Jewish—are judged for their actions over the previous year, and their reward or punishment designated.

The *Unetanah Tokef* is the central poem of the High Holy Days. The liturgy te3lls us, one Rosh Hashanah we are inscribed into the book of life, while on Yom Kippur, the book is sealed. These simple lines open us up to the possibility of teshuvah (repentance) and reflection of our past deeds.

"On Rosh Hashanah it is inscribed, and on Yom Kippur it is sealed.
How many shall pass away and how many shall be born,
Who shall live and who shall die,
Who shall reach the end of his days and who shall not,
Who shall perish by water and who by fire,
Who by sword and who by wild beast,
Who by famine and who by thirst,
Who by earthquake and who by plague,
Who by strangulation and who by stoning,
Who shall be at peace and who shall be pursued,
Who shall be exalted and who shall be brought low,
Who shall become rich and who shall be impoverished.
But repentance, prayer and righteousness avert the severe decree."

It is the day on which God inscribes the fate of each person in either the "Book of Life" or the "Book of Death," determining both if they will have a good or bad year and whether individuals will live or die. People who fall between the two categories have until Yom Kippur to perform "Teshuvah," or repentance. As a result, observant Jews consider Rosh Hashanah and the days surrounding it a time for prayer, good deeds, reflecting on past mistakes and making amends with others.

The sounding of the shofar—a trumpet made from a ram's horn—is an essential and emblematic part of both Rosh Hashanah and Yom Kippur. The ancient instrument's plaintive cry serves as a call to repentance and a reminder to Jews that God is their king. Tradition requires the shofar blower to play four sets of notes on Rosh Hashanah: tekiah, a long blast; shevarim, three short blasts; teruah, nine staccato blasts; and tekiah gedolah, a very long blast. Because of this ritual's close association with Rosh Hashanah, the holiday is also known as Yom Teruah—the day of the sounding of the shofar. The shofar is mindful of the biblical story of Abraham binding his son Isaac when a ram was caught in the thicket and sacrificed in Isaac's place. We blow a ram's horn to recall the great act of faith in God performed by Abraham and Isaac; tradition records that this event occurred on the day of Rosh Hashanah.

The shofar is not blown when Rosh Hashanah falls on Shabbat.

Customs and Symbols of Rosh Hashanah

- ✡ **Apples and honey:** One of the most popular Rosh Hashanah customs involves eating apple slices dipped in honey, sometimes after saying a special prayer. Ancient Jews believed apples had healing properties, and the honey signifies the hope that the new year will be sweet. Rosh Hashanah meals usually include an assortment of sweet treats for the same reason.

- ✡ **Round challah:** On Shabbat (the Jewish Sabbath) and other holidays, Jews eat loaves of the traditional braided bread known as challah. On Rosh Hashanah, the challah is often baked in a round shape to symbolize either the cyclical nature of life or the crown of God. Raisins are sometimes added to the dough for a sweet new year.

- ✡ **Tashlich:** On Rosh Hashanah, some Jews practice a custom known as tashlich ("casting off"), in which they throw pieces of bread into a flowing body of water while reciting prayers. As the bread, which symbolizes the sins of the past year, is swept away, those who embrace this tradition are spiritually cleansed and renewed.

✡ **"L'Shana Tovah":** Jews greet each other on Rosh Hashanah with the Hebrew phrase "L'Shana Tova", which translates to "for a good year."

Yom Kippur

The 10-day period known as the "Days of Awe" or the "Ten Days of Repentance" begins with Rosh Hashanah and ends with Yom Kippur. The time between these two main holidays is special in the Jewish calendar because Jews focus intently on repentance and atonement. While God passes judgment on Rosh Hashanah, the books of life and death remain open during the Days of Awe so that Jews can change which book they are in before it is sealed on Yom Kippur. Jews spend these days working to amend their behavior and seeking forgiveness for wrongs done during the past year.

The Shabbat that falls during this period is ascribed special importance as a day during which Jews can reflect on their mistakes and focus on repentance even more than on the other "Days of Awe" between Rosh Hashanah and Yom Kippur.

Often referred to as the "Day of Atonement," Yom Kippur is the holiest day in the Jewish calendar and concludes the period of the High Holidays and 10 "Days of Awe." The focus of the holiday is on repentance, and final atonement before the books of life and death are sealed.

As part of this day of atonement, adult Jews who are physically able to are required to fast for the entire day and abstain from other forms of pleasure (such as wearing leather, washing, and wearing perfumes). Most Jews, even many secular Jews, will attend prayer services for much of the day on Yom Kippur.

At the end of Yom Kippur, Jews who have atoned consider

themselves absolved of their sins from the previous year, thus beginning the new year with a clean slate in God's eyes and a renewed sense of purpose to live a more moral and just life in the year to come.

Yom Kippur takes its tone from the passage in Leviticus 16:29-30 mandating its observance: ***"It shall be a statute forever for you: in the seventh month, on the tenth day of the month, you shall afflict your souls and shall do no manner of work, the home-born nor the stranger that sojourns among you. For on this day shall atonement be made for you, to cleanse you; from all your sins before Adonai you shall be cleansed."***

All Jews over the age of thirteen are obliged to observe the fast. However, sick people not only may take their medications but are required to do so. Saving lives always takes precedence over other rules.

The fast serves several purposes:

1. It is a penance for our wrongdoing, a symbol of sacrifice that underlines our sense of remorse in God's eyes.

2. It is a display of our self-discipline, a sign of—perhaps to ourselves most of all—that we can control our appetites in all things.

3. The fast should help us to focus on the spiritual rather than the material, thinking not of business or food or drink, but of God and the sacred. We fast as if for one day we are angels, purely spiritual in nature.

4. Fasting is a way of awakening compassion in ourselves, making us experience for a single day the hunger that so many live with constantly.

As all holy days begin at sundown on the evening before, Yon Kippur begins with Kol Nidre. The service is named for the prayer that is perhaps the most famous and most beloved in all Jewish liturgy. It has a beautiful, plaintive melody accompanying very moving words. *Kol Nidre* means "all vows." The prayer asks God to forgive us for any vows made to Him that we have not been able to fulfill. It does not release one from promises made to others. Such promises must be settled between the parties themselves.

The theme that permeates not only Yom Kippur, but all the ten days, is that of reconciliation between people as a necessary prelude to reconciliation with God. The asking of forgiveness must be accompanied by some form of restitution and a resolution to do better in the future. The lesson of Yom Kippur is that the fast and prayer are acceptable to God only if they lead to good deeds. The four services on the day of Yom Kippur includes a litany of sins and confession of sins.

A memorial service for the dead is held as part of the day's service. The memory of loved ones is recalled in such prayers as:

"We remember all our beloved who have already reached the goal whither we are tending. We think of the days when they were with us, and we rejoice in the blessing of their companionship and affection. They are near us even now."

The concluding portion of the Yom Kippur service extols God's glory and his great mercy. As sunset approaches, the end of the day of prayer and fasting is announced by a blast of the shofar.

Sukkot

Sukkot or the Feast of Tabernacles (or Feast of Booths) is a week-long fall festival commemorating the 40-year journey of the Israelites in the wilderness. Along with Passover and the Festival of Weeks, Sukkot is one of three great pilgrimage feasts recorded in the Bible when all Jewish males were required to appear before the Lord in the Temple in Jerusalem.

The word *Sukkot* means «booths.» Throughout the holiday, Jews continue to observe this time by building and dwelling in temporary shelters, just like the Hebrew people did while wandering in the desert. This joyous celebration is a reminder of God›s deliverance, protection, provision, and faithfulness.

Sukkot begins five days after Yom Kippur, from the 15th-21st day of the Hebrew month of Tishri (September or October). See the Bible Feasts Calendar for the actual dates of Sukkot.

The observance of the Feast of Tabernacles is recorded in Exodus 23:16, 34:22; Leviticus 23:34-43; Numbers 29:12-40; Deuteronomy 16:13-15; Ezra 3:4; and Nehemiah 8:13-18.

The Bible reveals dual significance in the Feast of Tabernacles. Agriculturally, Sukkot is Israel's "Thanksgiving." It is a joyous harvest festival to celebrate the completion of the agricultural year. As a historical feast, its main characteristic is the requirement of Israel's people to leave their homes and to dwell in temporary shelters or booths. The Jews built these booths or tabernacles (temporary shelters) to commemorate their deliverance from Egypt and their protection, provision, and care by the hand of God during their 40 years in the wilderness.

As a feast instituted by God, Sukkot was never forgotten. It was celebrated in the time of Solomon (2 Chronicles 8:13). In fact, it was during Sukkot that Solomon's temple was dedicated (1 Kings 8:2). It was observed during Hezekiah's time (2 Chronicles 31:3; Deuteronomy16:16) and after the return from exile (Ezra 3:4; Zechariah 14:16,18-19).

Many interesting customs are associated with the celebration of Sukkot. The booth of Sukkot is called a *sukkah*. These shelters consist of at least three walls and are framed with wood and canvas. The roof or covering is made from cut branches and leaves, placed loosely atop, leaving open space for the stars to be viewed and rain to enter. It is common to decorate the sukkah with flowers, leaves, and fruits.

Today, the requirement to dwell in the booth can be met by eating at least one meal a day in it. However, some Jews still sleep in the sukkah. Since Sukkot is a harvest celebration, typical foods include lots of fresh fruits and vegetables.

During Sukkot, two important ceremonies took place. The Hebrew people carried torches around the temple, illuminating bright candelabrum along the walls of the temple to demonstrate that the Messiah would be a light to the Gentiles. Also, the priest would draw water from the pool of Siloam and carry it to the temple where it was poured into a silver basin beside the altar. The priest would call upon the Lord to provide heavenly water in the form of rain for their supply. During this ceremony, the people looked forward to the pouring out of the Holy Spirit. Some records reference the day spoken of by the prophet Joel.

In the New Testament, Jesus attended the Feast of Tabernacles and spoke these amazing words on the last and greatest day of the Feast: "If anyone is thirsty, let him come to me and drink. Whoever believes in me, as the Scripture has said, streams of living water will flow from within him." (John 7:37-38) The next morning, while the torches were still burning Jesus said, "I am the light of the world. Whoever follows me will never walk in darkness but will have the light of life." (John 8:12)

Chanukah

In the month of December, when Christians are celebrating the wondrous holiday of Christmas, the Jews are celebrating Chanukah. Chanukah is one of the most joyous and best-loved holidays. Unlike Christmas, which is a major holiday for Christians, Chanukah is a minor festival in the Jewish calendar.

Chanukah is a celebration of the Maccabees, Jewish warriors led by Judah Maccabee, who fought to recapture Jerusalem, overthrowing their Syrian oppressors and to reclaim the Temple for the Jewish people. Somewhere around 165 BC, the Maccabees continued to fight until they drove the Syrians from ancient Israel and reasserted Jewish sovereignty.

During the Syrian occupation of Jerusalem, the Temple was defiled by pagan sacrifices, on direct orders from the Syrian ruler, Antiochus Epiphanes. Those actions were the direct outcome of the stated Syrian policy of Hellenizing all of Palestine and eliminating the practice of the Jewish religion. When the Maccabees retook Jerusalem, they demolished the now polluted alter of the Temple and built a new one. They discarded the defiled ritual objects and replaced them.

They even found a small quantity of consecrated oil for use in the sacred lamps, but not nearly enough to use for the eight days of celebration and rededication. The priests lit the oil for the first day's worship. Miraculously, the next day there was enough for the second day's services. And so, it continued until the entire eight days of worship has been observed, with one day's worth of oil lasting the entire time. It is in honor of the miracle that Chanukah is observed with the lighting of the festival candles over the eight days of the holiday. Chanukah is Judaism's first post-biblical holiday. One not found in the Tanakh—the Hebrew bible.

It should be made clear that Chanukah is not the Jewish

Christmas. This mid-winter holiday became a sort of Jewish counterpart to Christmas, if only as a marketing ploy. In Israel the holiday has taken on an added symbolism, becoming a celebration of Jewish military prowess and national rebirth.

Customs and Symbols of Chanukah

✡ The principal observance of Chanukah takes place in the home. The central event of each evening of the holiday is the lighting of the Chanukah candles. These are placed in a menorah with nine candleholders. In addition to the eight candles representing each of the eight days of the festival, there is a place for a ninth candle which is used to kindle the other candles each night. The Chanukah candles are lit immediately after dark, with the exception of Friday nights, when they are lit before the Shabbat candles before sundown. The candles are placed in the menorah from right to left, then lit from left to right, so that the latest addition is placed last but lit first.

✡ Gifts are exchanged. Traditionally, children receive a simple gift each day. The giving of gifts at Chanukah is a recent custom, an attempt to keep up with the commercialization of Christmas.

✡ A favorite treat at Chanukah parties are *latkes* (potato pancakes). These pancakes are made from one's favorite recipe and handed down from generation to generation. The latkes are fried in oil to recall the miraculous oil that burned for eight days. They are served with sour cream or applesauce.

✡ The game of dreidel is played with a four-sided top with

a Hebrew letter on each side. The letters correspond to the first letter in each word of the saying, "A Great Miracle Happened There."

✡ *Tzedakah* (charity) is collected for the poor.

In the post-holocaust years, Chanukah has become very important to adults as well as to children. Its theme of religious freedom has taken on a deeper meaning. It symbolizes the triumph of faith in God over force: ***Not by might, nor by power, but My Spirit, saith the Lord of Hosts (Zechariah 4:6).*** It commemorates the first uprising in history for the sake of freedom of religion.

Chanukah is often called the Festival of Lights. One of the prayers in the synagogue service is: *"Let the lights we kindle shine forth for the world. May they illumine our lives even as they fill us with gratitude that our faith has been saved from extinction time and time again."*

Passover

Historically, together with Shavuot and Sukkot, Passover is one of the Three Pilgrimage Festivals during which the entire population of the kingdom of Judah made a pilgrimage to the Temple in Jerusalem.

Passover, also called *Pesach* is a major, biblically derived Jewish holiday. Jews celebrate Passover as a commemoration of their liberation by God from slavery in ancient Egypt and their freedom as a nation under the leadership of Moses. It commemorates the story of the Exodus as described in the Hebrew Bible, especially in the Book of Exodus, in which the Israelites were freed from slavery in Egypt. According to standard biblical chronology, this event would have taken place at about 1300 BC

Passover is a spring festival which during the existence of the Temple in Jerusalem was connected to the offering of the "first-fruits of the barley", barley being the first grain to ripen and to be harvested in the Land of Israel.

Passover commences on the 15th of the Hebrew month of Nisan and lasts for either seven days (in Israel and for Reform Jews and other progressive Jews around the world who adhere to the Biblical commandment) or eight days for Orthodox, and most Conservative Jews. In Judaism, a day commences at dusk and lasts until the following dusk, thus the first day of Passover begins after dusk of the 14th of Nisan and ends at dusk of the 15th day of the month of Nisan. The rituals unique to the Passover celebrations commence with the Passover Seder when the 15th of Nisan has begun. In the Northern Hemisphere Passover takes place in spring as the Torah prescribes it: **"in the month of the spring" (Exodus 23:15)**. It is one of the most widely celebrated Jewish holidays.

In the narrative of the Exodus, the Bible tells that God helped the Children of Israel escape from their slavery in Egypt by inflicting ten plagues upon the ancient Egyptians before the Pharaoh would release his Israelite slaves; the tenth and worst of the plagues was the death of the Egyptian first-born.

The Israelites were instructed to mark the doorposts of their homes with the blood of a slaughtered spring lamb and, upon seeing this, the spirit of the Lord knew to *pass over* the first-born in these homes, hence the English name of the holiday.

When the Pharaoh freed the Israelites, it is said that they left in such a hurry that they could not wait for bread dough to rise (leaven). In commemoration, for the duration of Passover, no leavened bread is eaten, for which reason Passover is called the Feast of Unleavened Bread in the Torah. Thus *matzoh* (flat unleavened bread) is eaten during Passover and it is a tradition of the holiday. More than that, they are instructed to clean their houses of all *chametz*—leavened bread or food made from wheat, barley, rye, spelt, and oats for the duration of the holiday.

One must not only abstain from eating leaven, one must not own any leaven. Prior to Passover, a Jew will "sell" all their leaven to a non-Jewish friend or neighbor. It has become a recent tradition to donate all leaven to food pantries in the neighborhood.

The matzah, the unleavened bread that Jews eat during the holiday, is at once a symbol of both freedom and, at the same time, of slavery. On the one hand, as Exodus 12:39 says, the Israelites "baked unleavened cakes of dough which they brought forth from Egypt … for they had been driven out of Egypt and could not delay…"

The Seder

It is traditional for Jewish families to gather on the first night of Passover for a special dinner called a seder derived from the Hebrew word for "order" or "arrangement", referring to the very specific order of the ritual meal. The table is set with the finest china and silverware to reflect the importance of the meal. During this meal, the story of the Exodus from Egypt is retold using a special text called the Haggadah. Four cups of wine are consumed at various stages in the narrative. The Haggadah divides the night's procedure into 15 parts, which parallel the 15 steps in the Temple in Jerusalem on which the Levites stood during Temple services, and which were memorialized in the 15 Psalms (120–134) known as Songs of Ascent".

The entire seder is heavy with meaning. The word seder literally means "order" and the seder is nothing if not orderly. At the center of the table is the seder plate, which holds a hard-boiled egg, a roasted bone, *maror*/bitter herbs, *charoset* (a mixture of chopped apples, nuts, cinnamon, wine, and honey), *karpas*/spring greens (usually parsley), and a small cup or saucer of saltwater. In addition, there is a plate holding three *matzahs*, covered with a cloth. Everyone at the table will have a *Haggadah*/the telling, the book containing the special liturgy for the evening meal.

The fifteen elements occur in a prescribed order:

1. *Kadesh:* The seder opens with the recitation of the festival *kiddush* over a glass of wine. Everyone drinks their first of four glasses of wine.

2. *Urkhatz:* The ritual washing of the hands, as in the handwashing before eating bread, but without the blessing.

3. *Karpas:* They leafy greens are dipped in the saltwater and, after the blessing for *karpas* is recited, they are eaten.

4. *Yakhatz: The* middle *matzah* from the center of the table is broken in half. One portion will be hidden for the afikomen, to be eaten at the very end of the meal. The tradition is for the host to hide it and for the children to search for it, ransoming it back to the leader at the end of the meal.

5. *Maggid:* The first part of the *Haggadah* is now read. This section of the seder includes the Four Questions, the list of the ten plagues, the story of the Exodus, an explanation of the significance of the Paschal lamb, *matzah, maror,* the first part of *Hallel,* and the second glass of wine.

6. *Rakhtsah:* Again, the hands are washed, this time with the blessing recited.

7. *Motzi:* The blessing for eating bread.

8. *Matzah:* The blessing for the unleavened bread.

9. *Maror:* The bitter herb is dipped in the *charoset* and eaten, with an appropriate blessing.

10. *Korekh:* A sandwich of bitter herb and *charoset* on *matzah* is eaten.

11. *Shukhan Orekh:* Dinner is served and eaten, a full and festive meal.

12. *Tsafun:* The *afikomen*, representing the Paschal sacrifice, is ransomed and eaten, officially ending the meal. After this, no more food should be eaten.

13. *Barekh:* Grace after meals is recited.

14. *Hallel:* The remainder of the *Hallel* psalms are recited.

15. *Nirtzah:* The celebration is "accepted," and those assembled declare, "Next year in Jerusalem."

A seder is a joyous occasion, a gathering of family and friends that should include not only the recitation of the *Haggadah*, but a spirited discussion with many questions and debate of the meaning of the holiday.

Passover and the seder are rich with symbolism. The *Haggadah* itself is largely occupied with explaining the significance of the elements of the seder. Certainly, the symbolic nature of the *maror* and the saltwater are obvious—the bitterness of slavery and the tears of the Israelites. The *charoset* relates to the mortar from which the Jewish slaves made bricks for the Pharaoh's cities, and the shank bone echoes the Paschal lambs' blood wit which Israelites marked the lintels of their doorways, signaling their presence to the Angel of Death so that he would *pass* over their homes and not take their first-born.

The *Haggadah* is very explicit that one is to retell the story of the Exodus as if we, ourselves, had been liberated from slavery in Egypt. Indeed, this idea is conveyed emphatically at several points in the text, echoing the words of the *Shema* (See page 39), "I am Adonai you God, who brought you out of Egypt to be your God," words that Jews all over the world repeat each day.

In the same prayer, we are instructed to teach the word "to your children," or as the phrase goes that recurs throughout Jewish liturgy, *"l'dor v'dor / from generation to generation."* Hence the enormous importance of children in Passover observance.

The Four Questions are asked by the youngest child at the table dealing with "Why is this night different?" By asking these questions, the youngest child allows an adult at the table to explain each of these practices and thereby to fulfill the obligation to tell the story to one's children.

The number four recurs throughout the *seder*. In addition to the Four Questions, we drink four glasses of wine. The most compelling explanation is that the four glasses represent the four promises God made to the Israelites in Exodus 6: "I will liberate you…I will deliver you…I will redeem you…I will take you to me as a people."

The strongest evidence for the interpretation is the custom of reserving a glass of wine at the table for the prophet Elijah, who returning to earth will herald the coming of the Messianic Age, a time of peace and prosperity for all. The hope of his coming is nothing less than an expression of the belief in the Creator's promise of a final redemption of *Olam Ha*-Ba/the World to Come. This fifth cup of wine corresponds to the fifth promise of Exodus, "…and I will bring you to the land which I promised your fathers."

The Seder ritual, as it is practiced today, did not exist at the time of Jesus. It was only fully developed by the rabbis in the years following the destruction of the Temple in 70 AD, in other words, at least two generations after Jesus. Many assume that Jesus, at the Last Supper, conducted what we now know of as a traditional Passover Seder with the Pesach (pascal) offering of the lamb, matzah, bitter herbs, the telling of the tale of the Exodus from Egypt, and other rituals as found in the Jewish Passover Haggadah. This is incorrect. Jesus certainly celebrated Passover, but the ritual Seder came along much later.

Shavuot

Shavuot is the third Pilgrimage Festival. Shavuot means "weeks" in Hebrew and is called the Feast of Weeks because it occurs seven weeks after the second day of Passover. It is also referred to as Pentecost, the fiftieth day after Passover. The Torah was given by God to the Jewish people on Mount Sinai on Shavuot more than 3,300 years ago. There are exactly fifty days, seven full weeks, from the second night of Passover to Shavuot. The counting of the days is to express the eagerness of the Jewish people freed from bondage in Egypt, to receive the Torah at Sinai. It is a bridge between the celebration of freedom to the celebration of the law. Every year on the holiday of Shavuot we renew our acceptance of God's gift.

Shavuot celebrates the most important moment in God's covenant with his people: the giving of the Torah to Moses and its acceptance by the Jews at Sinai. It is clear from all Torah commentaries and explanatory stories that the acceptance of the Ten Commandments and the Torah that contains them is at the heart of any concept of Jewish uniqueness and historical mission. If ethical monotheism is the central concept of Judaism, Torah is the center of ethical monotheism, and almost everything Jews believe proceeds from Torah directly or indirectly.

Shavuot has come to be dedicated to the idea of Torah study and Jewish education. In the synagogue, the Book of Ruth is read. One custom that traditional Jews still observe is an all-night study session held on the first evening of the festival.

Purim

Purim is one of the most joyous and fun holidays on the Jewish calendar. It commemorates a time when the Jewish people living in Persia were saved from extermination.

The story of Purim is told in the Biblical book of Esther. The heroes of the story are Esther, a beautiful young Jewish woman living in Persia, and her cousin Mordecai, who raised her as if she were his daughter. Esther was taken to the house of Ahasuerus, King of Persia, to become part of his harem. King Ahasuerus loved Esther more than his other women and made Esther queen, but the king did not know that Esther was a Jew, because Mordecai told her not to reveal her identity.

The villain of the story is Haman, an arrogant, egotistical advisor to the king. Haman hated Mordecai because Mordecai refused to bow down to Haman, so Haman plotted to destroy the Jewish people. In a speech that is all too familiar to Jews, Haman told the king, **"Then Haman said to King Ahasuerus, "There is a certain people scattered and separated among the peoples in all the provinces of your kingdom; their laws are different from those of every other people, and they do not keep the king's laws, so that it is not appropriate for the king to tolerate them." (Esther 3:8).** The king gave the fate of the Jewish people to Haman, to do as he pleased to them. Haman planned to exterminate all the Jews.

Mordecai persuaded Esther to speak to the king on behalf of the Jewish people. This was a dangerous thing for Esther to do because anyone who came into the king's presence without being summoned could be put to death, and she had not been summoned. Esther fasted for three days to prepare herself, then went into the king. He welcomed her. Later, she told him of Haman's plot against her people. The Jewish people were saved, and Haman and his ten sons were hanged on the gallows that had been prepared for Mordecai.

The book of Esther is unusual in that it is the only book of the Bible that does not contain the name of God. In fact, it includes virtually no reference to God.

Tisha B'av

Tisha B'Av, the Fast of the Ninth of Av, is a day of mourning to commemorate the many tragedies that have befallen the Jewish people, many of which coincidentally occurred on the ninth of Av. Tisha B'Av literally means "the ninth day of Av" in Hebrew. It usually occurs during August.

Tisha B'Av primarily commemorates the destruction of Solomon's Temple by the Babylonians in 423 BC and the Second Temple, by the Romans in 70 AD

Although this holiday is primarily meant to commemorate the destruction of the Temple, it is appropriate to consider the many other tragedies of the Jewish people that also occurred on this day. Among them are: the crushing of the Bar-Kokhba Revolt at the hands of the Romans in 133 AD.; the expulsion of the Jews from England in 1290 AD; the expulsion of the Jews from Spain in 1492; and the beginning of World War I in 1914, which by general historical consensus led to World War II and the Holocaust.

The restrictions on Tisha B'Av are similar to those on Yom Kippur: to refrain from eating and drinking (even water), washing, bathing, shaving or wearing cosmetics, wearing leather shoes, and engaging in sexual relations. Work in the ordinary sense of the word is also restricted. People who are ill need not fast on this day. Many of the traditional mourning practices are observed: people refrain from smiles, laughter and idle conversation, and sit on low stools.

In Synagogue, the book of Lamentations is read, and mourning prayers are recited. The ark where the Torah is kept is draped in black.

APPENDIX

613 Commandments Sorted by Category

God

1.To know that God exists (Ex. 20:2; Deut. 5:6)

2.Not to entertain the idea that there is any god but the Eternal (Ex. 20:3)

3.Not to blaspheme (Ex. 22:27-28)

4.To hallow God's name (Lev. 22:32)

5.Not to profane God's name (Lev. 22:32

6.To know that God is One, a complete Unity (Deut. 6:4)

7.To love God (Deut. 6:5)

8.To fear Him reverently (Deut. 6:13; 10:20)

9.Not to put the word of God to the test (Deut. 6:16)

10.To imitate His good and upright ways (Deut. 28:9)

The Law

11.To honor the old and the wise (Lev. 19:32)

12.To learn Torah and to teach it (Deut. 6:7)

13.To cleave to those who know Him (Deut. 10:20)

14.Not to add to the commandments of the Torah. (Deut.13:1)

15.Not to take away from the commandments of the Torah (Deut.13:1)

16.That every person shall write a scroll of the Torah for himself (Deut. 31:19)

Signs and Symbols

17.To circumcise the male offspring (Gen. 17:12; Lev. 12:3)

18.To put fringes on the corners of clothing (Num. 15:38)

19.To bind God's Word on the head (Deut. 6:8)

20.To bind God's Word on the arm (Deut. 6:8)

21.To affix the mezuzah to the door posts and gates of your house (Deut. 6:9)

Prayer and Blessing

22.To pray to God (Ex. 23:25; Deut. 6:13)

23.To read the Shema [lit: The Hearing] in the morning and at night (Deut. 6:7)

24.To recite grace after meals (Deut. 8:10)

25.Not to lay down a stone for worship (Lev. 26:1)

Love and Brotherhood

26.To love all human beings who are of the covenant (Lev. 19:18)

27.Not to stand by idly when a human life is in danger (Lev. 19:16)

28.Not to wrong any one in speech (Lev. 25:17)

29.Not to carry tales (Lev. 19:16)

30.Not to cherish hatred in one's heart (Lev. 19:17)

31.Not to take revenge (Lev. 19:18)

32.Not to bear a grudge (Lev. 19:18)

33.Not to put any Jew to shame (Lev. 19:17)

34.Not to curse any other Israelite (Lev. 19:14)

35.Not to give occasion to the simple-minded to stumble on the road (Lev. 19:14) (this includes doing anything that will cause another to sin)

36.To rebuke the sinner (Lev. 19:17)

37.To relieve a neighbor of his burden and help to unload his beast (Ex. 23:5)

38.To assist in replacing the load upon a neighbor's beast (Deut.22:4)

39.Not to leave a beast, that has fallen beneath its burden, unaided (Deut. 22:4)

The Poor and Unfortunate

40. Not to afflict an orphan or a widow (Ex. 22:21)

41. Not to reap the entire field (Lev. 19:9; Lev. 23:22)

42. To leave the unreaped corners of the field or orchard for the poor (Lev. 19:9)

43. Not to gather gleanings (the ears that have fallen to the ground while reaping) (Lev. 19:9)

44. To leave the gleanings for the poor (Lev. 19:9)

45. Not to gather ol'loth (the imperfect clusters) of the vineyard (Lev. 19:10)

46. To leave ol'loth (the imperfect clusters) of the vineyard for the poor (Lev. 19:10; Deut. 24:21)

47. Not to gather the single grapes that have fallen to the ground (Lev. 19:10)

48. To leave the single grapes of the vineyard for the poor (Lev. 19:10)

49. Not to return to take a forgotten sheaf (Deut. 24:19) This applies to all fruit trees (Deut. 24:20)

50. To leave the forgotten sheaves for the poor (Deut. 24:19-20)

51. Not to refrain from maintaining a poor man and giving him what he needs (Deut. 15:7)

52. To give charity according to one's means (Deut. 15:11) Treatment of the Gentiles

53. To love the stranger (Deut. 10:19) (CCA61).

54. Not to wrong the stranger in speech (Ex. 22:20)

55. Not to wrong the stranger in buying or selling (Ex. 22:20).

56. Not to intermarry with gentiles (Deut. 7:3)

57. To exact the debt of an alien (Deut. 15:3)

58. To lend to an alien at interest (Deut. 23:21)

Marriage, Divorce and Family

59. To honor father and mother (Ex. 20:12)

60. Not to smite a father or a mother (Ex. 21:15)

61. Not to curse a father or mother (Ex. 21:17)

62. To reverently fear father and mother (Lev. 19:3)

63. To be fruitful and multiply (Gen. 1:28)

64. That a eunuch shall not marry a daughter of Israel (Deut. 23:2)

65. That a bastard [Heb. mamzer = illegitimate son] shall not marry the daughter of a Jew (Deut.23:3)

66. That an Ammonite or Moabite shall never marry the daughter of an Israelite (Deut. 23:4)

67. Not to exclude a descendant of Esau from the community of Israel for three generations (Deut. 23:8-9)

68. Not to exclude an Egyptian from the community of Israel for three generations (Deut. 23:8-9)

69. That there shall be no harlot (in Israel); that is, that there shall be no intercourse with a woman, without previous marriage with a deed of marriage and formal declaration of marriage (Deut.23:18)

70. To take a wife by the sacrament of marriage (Deut.24:1)

71. That the newly married husband shall (be free) for one year to rejoice with his wife (Deut. 24:5)

72. That a bridegroom shall be exempt for a whole year from taking part in any public labor, such as military service, guarding the wall and similar duties (Deut. 24:5)

73. Not to withhold food, clothing or conjugal rights from a wife (Ex. 21:10)

74. That the woman suspected of adultery shall be dealt with as prescribed in the Torah (Num. 5:30)

75. That one who defames his wife's honor (by falsely accusing her of

unchastity before marriage) must live with her all his lifetime (Deut. 22:19)

76.That a man may not divorce his wife concerning whom he has published an evil report (about her unchastity before marriage) (Deut. 22:19)

77.To divorce by a formal written document (Deut. 24:1)

78.That one who divorced his wife shall not remarry her, if after the divorce she had been married to another man (Deut. 24:4)

79.That a widow whose husband died childless must not be married to anyone but her deceased husband's brother (Deut. 25:5) (this is only in effect insofar as it requires the procedure of release below).

80.To marry the widow of a brother who has died childless (Deut.25:5) (this is only in effect insofar as it requires the procedure of release below)

81.That the widow formally releases the brother-in-law (if he refuses to marry her) (Deut. 25:7-9)

Forbidden Sexual Relations

82.Not to indulge in familiarities with relatives, such as sensual kissing, carnal embracing, or provocative winking which may lead to incest (Lev.18:6)

83.Not to commit incest with one's mother (Lev. 18:7)

84.Not to commit sodomy with one's father (Lev. 18:7)

85.Not to commit incest with one's father's wife (Lev. 18:8)

86.Not to commit incest with one's sister (Lev. 18:9)

87.Not to commit incest with one's father's wife's daughter (Lev.18:9)

88.Not to commit incest with one's son's daughter (Lev. 18:10)

89.Not to commit incest with one's daughter's daughter (Lev.18:10)

90.Not to commit incest with one's daughter (this is not explicitly in the Torah but is inferred from other explicit commands that would include it)

91.Not to commit incest with one's father's sister (Lev. 18:12)

92.Not to commit incest with one's mother's sister (Lev. 18:13)

93.Not to commit incest with one's father's brother's wife (Lev.18:14)

94.Not to commit sodomy with one's father's brother (Lev. 18:14)

95.Not to commit incest with one's son's wife (Lev. 18:15)

96.Not to commit incest with one's brother's wife (Lev. 18:16)

97.Not to commit incest with one's wife's daughter (Lev. 18:17)

98.Not to commit incest with the daughter of one's wife's son (Lev.18:17)

99.Not to commit incest with the daughter of one's wife's daughter (Lev. 18:17)

100.Not to commit incest with one's wife's sister (Lev. 18:18)

101.Not to have intercourse with a woman, in her menstrual period (Lev. 18:19)

102.Not to have intercourse with another man's wife (Lev. 18:20)

103.Not to commit sodomy with a male (Lev. 18:22) 104.Not to have intercourse with a beast (Lev. 18:23)

105.That a woman shall not have intercourse with a beast (Lev.18:23)

106.Not to castrate the male of any species; neither a man, nor a domestic or wild beast, nor a fowl (Lev. 22:24)

Times and Seasons

107.That the new month shall be solemnly proclaimed as holy, and the months and years shall be calculated by the Supreme Court only (Ex. 12:2)

108.Not to travel on the Sabbath outside the limits of one's place of residence (Ex. 16:29)

109.To sanctify the Sabbath (Ex. 20:8)

110.Not to do work on Sabbath (Ex. 20:10)

111.To rest on Sabbath (Ex. 23:12; 34:21)

112.To celebrate the festivals (Ex.23:14)

113.To rejoice on the festivals (Deut. 16:14)

114.To appear in the Sanctuary on the festivals (Deut. 16:16)

115.To remove leaven on the Eve of Passover (Ex. 12:15)

116.To rest on the first day of Passover (Ex. 12:16; Lev. 23:7)

117.Not to do work on the first day of Passover (Ex. 12:16; Lev.23:6-7)

118.To rest on the seventh day of Passover (Ex. 12:16; Lev. 23:8)

119.Not to do work on the seventh day of Passover (Ex. 12:16; Lev. 23:8)

120.To eat "matzah" [unleavened bread] on the first night of Passover (Ex. 12:18)

121.That no leaven be in the Israelite's possession during Passover (Ex. 12:19)

122.Not to eat any food containing leaven on Passover (Ex.12:20)

123.Not to eat leaven on Passover (Ex. 13:3)

124.That leaven shall not be seen in an Israelite's home during Passover (Ex. 13:7)

125.To discuss the departure from Egypt on the first night of Passover (Ex. 13:8)

126.Not to eat leaven after mid-day on the fourteenth of Nissan (Deut. 16:3)

127.To count forty-nine days from the time of the cutting of the Omer (i.e. first sheaves of the barley harvest) (Lev. 23:15)

128.To rest on Pentecost (Lev. 23:21)

129.Not to do work on the feast of Pentecost (Lev. 23:21)

130.To rest on Rosh Hashanah [i.e. the feast of Trumpets] (Lev. 23:24)

131.Not to do work on Rosh Hashanah (Lev. 23:25)

132.To hear the sound of the Trumpet [Heb. shofar or ram's horn] (Num.29:1)

133. To fast on Yom Kippur i.e. the day of Atonement (Lev. 23:27)

134. Not to eat or drink on Yom Kippur (Lev. 23:29)

135. Not to do work on Yom Kippur (Lev. 23:31

136. To rest on the Yom Kippur (Lev. 23:32)

137. To rest on the first day of the feast of Tabernacles or Booths. [Heb. Sukkot] (Lev. 23:35)

138. Not to do work on the first day of the feast of Tabernacles. (Lev. 23:35)

139. To rest on the eighth day of the feast of Tabernacles (Lev.23:36)

140. Not to do work on the eighth day of the feast of Tabernacles (Lev. 23:36)

141. To take during Sukkot a palm branch and the other three plants (Lev. 23:40)

142. To dwell in booths seven days during Sukkot (Lev. 23:42)

Dietary Laws

143. To examine the marks in cattle (so as to distinguish the clean from the unclean) (Lev. 11:2)

144. Not to eat the flesh of unclean beasts (Lev. 11:4)

145. To examine the marks in fishes (so as to distinguish the clean from the unclean (Lev. 11:9)

146. Not to eat unclean fish (Lev. 11:11)

147. To examine the marks in fowl, so as to distinguish the clean from the unclean (Deut. 14:11)

148. Not to eat unclean fowl (Lev. 11:13)

149. To examine the marks in locusts, so as to distinguish the clean from the unclean (Lev. 11:21)

150. Not to eat a worm found in fruit (Lev. 11:41)

151. Not to eat of things that creep upon the earth (Lev. 11:41-42)

152. Not to eat any vermin of the earth (Lev. 11:44)

153.Not to eat things that swarm in the water (Lev. 11:43 and 46)

154.Not to eat of winged insects (Deut. 14:19)

155.Not to eat the flesh of a beast that is torn (Ex.22:30)

156.Not to eat the flesh of a beast that died of itself (Deut. 14:21)

157.To slay cattle, deer and fowl according to the law if their flesh is to be eaten (Deut. 12:21)

158.Not to eat a limb removed from a living beast (Deut. 12:23)

159.Not to slaughter an animal and its young on the same day (Lev.22:28)

160.Not to take the mother-bird with the young (Deut. 22:6)

161.To set the mother-bird free when taking the nest (Deut.22:6-7)

162.Not to eat the flesh of an ox that was condemned to be stoned (Ex. 21:28)

163.Not to boil meat with milk (Ex. 23:19)

164.Not to eat flesh with milk (Ex. 34:26)

165.Not to eat the of the thigh-vein which shrank (Gen. 32:33)

166.Not to eat the fat of the offering (Lev. 7:23)

167.Not to eat blood (Lev. 7:26)

168.To cover the blood of undomesticated animals (deer, etc.) and of fowl that have been killed (Lev. 17:13)

169.Not to eat or drink like a glutton or a drunkard (not to rebel against father or mother) (Lev. 19:26; Deut. 21:20)

Business Practices

170.Not to do wrong in buying or selling (Lev. 25:14)

171.Not to make a loan to an Israelite on interest (Lev. 25:37)

172.Not to borrow on interest (Deut. 23:20) (because this would cause the lender to sin)

173.Not to take part in any usurious transaction between borrower and lender, neither as a surety, nor as a witness, nor as a writer of the bond for them (Ex. 22:24)

174. To lend to a poor person (Ex. 22:24)

175. Not to demand from a poor man repayment of his debt, when the creditor knows that he cannot pay, nor press him (Ex.22:24)

176. Not to take in pledge utensils used in preparing food (Deut.24:6)

177. Not to exact a pledge from a debtor by force (Deut. 24:10)

178. Not to keep the pledge from its owner at the time when he needs it (Deut. 24:12)

179. To return a pledge to its owner (Deut. 24:13)

180. Not to take a pledge from a widow (Deut. 24:17)

181. Not to commit fraud in measuring (Lev. 19:35)

182. To ensure that scales and weights are correct (Lev. 19:36)

183. Not to possess inaccurate measures and weights (Deut.25:13-14)

Employees, Servants and Slaves

184. Not to delay payment of a hired man's wages (Lev. 19:13)

185. That the hired laborer shall be permitted to eat of the produce he is reaping (Deut. 23:25-26)

186. That the hired laborer shall not take more than he can eat (Deut. 23:25)

187. That a hired laborer shall not eat produce that is not being harvested (Deut. 23:26)

188. To pay wages to the hired man at the due time (Deut. 24:15)

189. To deal judicially with the Hebrew bondman in accordance with the laws appertaining to him (Ex. 21:2-6)

190. Not to compel the Hebrew servant to do the work of a slave (Lev. 25:39)

191. Not to sell a Hebrew servant as a slave (Lev. 25:42)

192. Not to treat a Hebrew servant rigorously (Lev. 25:43)

193. Not to permit a gentile to treat harshly a Hebrew bondman sold to him (Lev. 25:53)

194.Not to send away a Hebrew bondman servant empty handed, when he is freed from service (Deut. 15:13)

195.To bestow liberal gifts upon the Hebrew bondsman (at the end of his term of service), and the same should be done to a Hebrew bondwoman (Deut. 15:14)

196.To redeem a Hebrew maid-servant (Ex. 21:8)

197.Not to sell a Hebrew maid-servant to another person (Ex. 21:8)

198.To espouse a Hebrew maid-servant (Ex. 21:8-9)

199.To keep the Canaanite slave forever (Lev. 25:46)

200.Not to surrender a slave, who has fled to the land of Israel, to his owner who lives outside Palestine (Deut. 23:16) 201.Not to wrong such a slave (Deut. 23:17)

202.Not to muzzle a beast, while it is working in produce which it can eat and enjoy (Deut. 25:4)

Vows, Oaths and Swearing

203.That a man should fulfill whatever he has uttered (Deut. 23:24)

204.Not to swear needlessly (Ex. 20:7)

205.Not to violate an oath or swear falsely (Lev. 19:12)

206.To decide in cases of annulment of vows, according to the rules set forth in the Torah (Num. 30:2-17)

207.Not to break a vow (Num. 30:3)

208.To swear by His name truly (Deut. 10:20)

209.Not to delay in fulfilling vows or bringing vowed or free-will offerings (Deut. 23:22)

The Sabbatical and Jubilee Years

210.To let the land lie fallow in the Sabbatical year (Ex. 23:11; Lev.25:2)

211.To cease from tilling the land in the Sabbatical year (Ex. 23:11) (Lev. 25:2)

212.Not to till the ground in the Sabbatical year (Lev. 25:4)

213.Not to do any work on the trees in the Sabbatical year (Lev.25:4)

214.Not to reap the aftermath that grows in the Sabbatical year, in the same way as it is reaped in other years (Lev. 25:5)

215.Not to gather the fruit of the tree in the Sabbatical year in the same way as it is gathered in other years (Lev. 25:5) 216.To sound the Ram's horn in the Sabbatical year (Lev. 25:9)

217.To release debts in the seventh year (Deut. 15:2)

218.Not to demand return of a loan after the Sabbatical year has passed (Deut. 15:2)

219.Not to refrain from making a loan to a poor man, because of the release of loans in the Sabbatical year (Deut. 15:9) 220.To assemble the people to hear the Torah at the close of the seventh year (Deut. 31:12)

221.To count the years of the Jubilee by years and by cycles of seven years (Lev. 25:8)

222.To keep the Jubilee year holy by resting and letting the land lie fallow (Lev. 25:10)

223.Not to cultivate the soil nor do any work on the trees, in the Jubilee Year (Lev. 25:11)

224.Not to reap the aftermath of the field that grew of itself in the Jubilee Year, in the same way as in other years (Lev. 25:11)

225.Not to gather the fruit of the tree in the Jubilee Year, in the same way as in other years (Lev. 25:11)

226.To grant redemption to the land in the Jubilee year (Lev. 25:24)

The Court and Judicial Procedure

227.To appoint judges and officers in every community of Israel (Deut. 16:18)

228.Not to appoint as a judge, a person who is not well versed in the laws of the Torah, even if he is expert in other branches of knowledge (Deut. 1:17)

229.To adjudicate cases of purchase and sale (Lev. 25:14)

230.To judge cases of liability of a paid depositary (Ex. 22:9)

231.To adjudicate cases of loss for which a gratuitous borrower is liable (Ex. 22:13-14)

232.To adjudicate cases of inheritances (Num. 27:8-11)

233.To judge cases of damage caused by an uncovered pit (Ex.21:33-34)

234.To judge cases of injuries caused by beasts (Ex. 21:35-36)

235.To adjudicate cases of damage caused by trespass of cattle (Ex.22:4)

236.To adjudicate cases of damage caused by fire (Ex. 22:5)

237.To adjudicate cases of damage caused by a gratuitous depositary (Ex. 22:6-7)

238.To adjudicate other cases between a plaintiff and a defendant (Ex. 22:8)

239.Not to curse a judge (Ex. 22:27)

240.That one who possesses evidence shall testify in Court (Lev.5:1)

241.Not to testify falsely (Ex. 20:13)

242.That a witness, who has testified in a capital case, shall not lay down the law in that particular case (Num. 35:30) 243.That a transgressor shall not testify (Ex. 23:1)

244.That the court shall not accept the testimony of a close relative of the defendant in matters of capital punishment (Deut. 24:16)

245.Not to hear one of the parties to a suit in the absence of the other party (Ex. 23:1)

246.To examine witnesses thoroughly (Deut. 13:15)

247.Not to decide a case on the evidence of a single witness (Deut.19:15)

248.To give the decision according to the majority, when there is a difference of opinion among the members of the Sanhedrin as to matters of law (Ex. 23:2)

249.Not to decide, in capital cases, according to the view of the majority, when those who are for condemnation exceed by one only, those who are for acquittal (Ex. 23:2)

250. That, in capital cases, one who had argued for acquittal, shall not later argue for condemnation (Ex. 23:2)

251. To treat parties in a litigation with equal impartiality (Lev. 19:15)

252. Not to render iniquitous decisions (Lev. 19:15)

253. Not to favor a great man when trying a case (Lev. 19:15)

254. Not to take a bribe (Ex. 23:8)

255. Not to be afraid of a bad man, when trying a case (Deut. 1:17)

256. Not to be moved in trying a case, by the poverty of one of the parties (Ex. 23:3; Lev. 19:15)

257. Not to pervert the judgment of strangers or orphans (Deut.24:17)

258. Not to pervert the judgment of a sinner (a person poor in fulfillment of commandments) (Ex. 23:6)

259. Not to render a decision on one's personal opinion, but only on the evidence of two witnesses, who saw what actually occurred (Ex. 23:7)

260. Not to execute one guilty of a capital offense, before he has stood his trial (Num. 35:12)

261. To accept the rulings of every Supreme Court in Israel (Deut.17:11)

262. Not to rebel against the orders of the Court (Deut. 17:11)

Injuries and Damages

263. To make a parapet for your roof (Deut. 22:8)

264. Not to leave something that might cause hurt (Deut. 22:8)

265. To save the pursued even at the cost of the life of the pursuer (Deut. 25:12)

266. Not to spare a pursuer, but he is to be slain before he reaches the pursued and slays the latter, or uncovers his nakedness (Deut. 25:12)

Property and Property Rights

267. Not to sell a field in the land of Israel in perpetuity (Lev. 25:23)

268. Not to change the character of the open land (about the cities of) the Levites or of their fields; not to sell it in perpetuity, but it may be redeemed at any time (Lev. 25:34)

269.That houses sold within a walled city may be redeemed within a year (Lev. 25:29)

270.Not to remove landmarks (property boundaries) (Deut. 19:14)

271.Not to swear falsely in denial of another's property rights (Lev.19:11)

272.Not to deny falsely another's property rights (Lev. 19:11)

273.Never to settle in the land of Egypt (Deut. 17:16)

274.Not to steal personal property (Lev. 19:11)

275.To restore that which one took by robbery (Lev. 5:23)

276.To return lost property (Deut. 22:1)

277.Not to pretend not to have seen lost property, to avoid the obligation to return it (Deut. 22:3) Criminal Laws 278.Not to slay an innocent person (Ex. 20:13)

279.Not to kidnap any person of Israel (Ex. 20:13)

280.Not to rob by violence (Lev. 19:13)

281.Not to defraud (Lev. 19:13)

282.Not to covet what belongs to another (Ex. 20:14)

283.Not to crave something that belongs to another (Deut. 5:18)

284.Not to indulge in evil thoughts and sights (Num. 15:39)

Punishment and Restitution

285.That the Court shall pass sentence of death by decapitation with the sword (Ex. 21:20; Lev. 26:25)

286.That the Court shall pass sentence of death by strangulation (Lev. 20:10)

287.That the Court shall pass sentence of death by burning with fire (Lev. 20:14)

288.That the Court shall pass sentence of death by stoning (Deut.22:24)

289.To hang the dead body of one who has incurred that penalty (Deut. 21:22)

290.That the dead body of an executed criminal shall not remain hanging on the tree overnight (Deut. 21:23)

291.To inter the executed on the day of execution (Deut. 21:23)

292.Not to accept ransom from a murderer (Num. 35:31)

293.To exile one who committed accidental homicide (Num. 35:25)

294.To establish six cities of refuge (for those who committed accidental homicide) (Deut. 19:3)

295.Not to accept ransom from an accidental homicide, so as to relieve him from exile (Num. 35:32)

296.To decapitate the heifer in the manner prescribed (in expiation of a murder on the road, the perpetrator of which remained undiscovered) (Deut. 21:4)

297.Not to plow nor sow the rough valley (in which a heifer's neck was broken) (Deut. 21:4)

298.To adjudge a thief to pay compensation or (in certain cases) suffer death (Ex. 21:16; Ex. 21:37; Ex. 22:1)

299.That he who inflicts a bodily injury shall pay monetary compensation (Ex. 21:18-19)

300.To impose a penalty of fifty shekels upon the seducer (of an unbetrothed virgin) and enforce the other rules in connection with the case (Ex. 22:15-16)

301.That the violator (of an unbetrothed virgin) shall marry her (Deut. 22:28-29)

302.That one who has raped a damsel and has then (in accordance with the law) married her, may not divorce her (Deut. 22:29)

303.Not to inflict punishment on the sabbath (Ex. 35:3) (because some punishments were inflicted by fire)

304.To punish the wicked by the infliction of stripes (Deut. 25:2)

305.Not to exceed the statutory number of stripes laid on one who has incurred that punishment (Deut. 25:3) (and by implication, not to strike anyone)

306.Not to spare the offender, in imposing the prescribed penalties on one who has caused damage (Deut. 19:13) 307.To do unto false witnesses as they had purposed to do (to the accused) (Deut. 19:19)

308.Not to punish anyone who has committed an offense under duress (Deut. 22:26)

Prophecy

309.To heed the call of every prophet in each generation, provided that he neither adds to, nor takes away from the Torah (Deut.18:15)

310.Not to prophesy falsely (Deut. 18:20)

311.Not to refrain from putting a false prophet to death nor to be in fear of him (Deut. 18:22) (negative)

Idolatry, Idolaters and Idolatrous Practices

312.Not to make a graven image; neither to make it oneself nor to have it made by others (Ex. 20:4)

313.Not to make any figures for ornament, even if they are not worshipped (Ex. 20:20)

314.Not to make idols even for others (Ex. 34:17; Lev. 19:4)

315.Not to use the ornament of any object of idolatrous worship (Deut. 7:25)

316.Not to make use of an idol or its accessory objects, offerings, or libations (Deut. 7:26)

317.Not to drink wine of idolaters (Deut. 32:38)

318.Not to worship an idol in the way in which it is usually worshipped (Ex. 20:5)

319.Not to bow down to an idol, even if that is not its mode of worship (Ex. 20:5)

320.Not to prophesy in the name of an idol (Ex. 23:13; Deut.18:20)

321.Not to hearken to one who prophesies in the name of an idol (Deut. 13:4)

322.Not to lead the children of Israel astray to idolatry (Ex. 23:13)

323.Not to entice an Israelite to idolatry (Deut. 13:12)

324.To destroy idolatry and its appurtenances (Deut. 12:2-3)

325.Not to love the enticer to idolatry (Deut. 13:9)

326.Not to give up hating the enticer to idolatry (Deut. 13:9)

327.Not to save the enticer from capital punishment, but to stand by at his execution (Deut. 13:9)

328.A person whom he attempted to entice to idolatry shall not urge pleas for the acquittal of the enticer (Deut. 13:9) 329.A person whom he attempted to entice shall not refrain from giving evidence of the enticer's guilt, if he has such evidence (Deut. 13:9)

330.Not to swear by an idol to its worshipers, nor cause them to swear by it (Ex. 23:13)

331.Not to turn one's attention to idolatry (Lev. 19:4)

332.Not to adopt the institutions of idolaters nor their customs (Lev. 18:3; Lev. 20:23)

333.Not to pass a child through the fire to Molech (Lev. 18:21)

334.Not to suffer anyone practicing witchcraft to live (Ex. 22:17)

335.Not to practice observing times or seasons -i.e. astrology (Lev. 19:26)

336.Not to practice superstitions/witchcraft (doing things based on signs and potions; using charms and incantations) (Lev. 19:26)

337.Not to consult familiar spirits or ghosts (Lev. 19:31)

338.Not to consult wizards (Lev. 19:31)

339.Not to practice specific magic by using stones herbs or objects. (Deut. 18:10)

340.Not to practice magical practices in general. (Deut. 18:10)

341.Not to practice the art of casting spells over snakes and scorpions (Deut. 18:11)

342.Not to enquire of a familiar spirit or ghost (Deut. 18:11)

343.Not to seek the dead (Deut. 18:11) 344.Not to enquire of a wizard) (Deut. 18:11)

345. Not to remove the entire beard, like the idolaters (Lev. 19:27)

346. Not to round the corners of the head, as the idolatrous priests do (Lev. 19:27)

347. Not to cut oneself or make incisions in one's flesh in grief, like the idolaters (Lev. 19:28; Deut. 14:1)

348. Not to tattoo the body like the idolaters (Lev. 19:28)

349. Not to make a bald spot for the dead (Deut. 14:1)

350. Not to plant a tree for worship (Deut. 16:21)

351. Not to set up a pillar (for worship) (Deut. 16:22) 352. Not to show favor to idolaters (Deut. 7:2)

353. Not to make a covenant with the seven (Canaanite, idolatrous) nations (Ex. 23:32; Deut. 7:2)

354. Not to settle idolaters in our land (Ex. 23:33)

355. To slay the inhabitants of a city that has become idolatrous and burn that city (Deut. 13:16-17)

356. Not to rebuild a city that has been led astray to idolatry (Deut. 13:17)

357. Not to make use of the property of city that has been so led astray (Deut. 13:18)

Agriculture and Animal Husbandry

358. Not to cross-breed cattle of different species (Lev. 19:19)

359. Not to sow different kinds of seed together in one field (Lev. 19:19)

360. Not to eat the fruit of a tree for three years from the time it was planted (Lev. 19:23)

361. That the fruit of fruit-bearing trees in the fourth year of their planting shall be sacred like the second tithe and eaten in Jerusalem (Lev. 19:24)

362. Not to sow grain or herbs in a vineyard (Deut. 22:9)

363. Not to eat the produce of diverse seeds sown in a vineyard (Deut. 22:9)

364. Not to work with beasts of different species, yoked together (Deut. 22:10)

Clothing

365. That a man shall not wear women's clothing (Deut. 22:5)

366. That a woman should not wear men's clothing (Deut. 22:5)

367. Not to wear garments made of wool and linen mixed together (Deut. 22:11)

The Firstborn

368. To redeem the firstborn human male (Ex. 13:13; Ex. 34:20; Num. 18:15)

369. To redeem the firstling of an ass (Ex. 13:13; Ex. 34:20)

370. To break the neck of the firstling of an ass if it is not redeemed (Ex. 13:13; Ex. 34:20)

371. Not to redeem the firstling of a clean beast (Num. 18:17)

High Priest, Priests and Levites

372. That the Priest shall put on priestly vestments for the service (Ex. 28:2)

373. Not to tear the High Priest's robe (Ex. 28:32)

374. That the Priest shall not enter the Sanctuary at all times (i.e., at times when he is not performing service) (Lev. 16:2) 375. That the ordinary Priest shall not defile himself by contact with any dead, other than immediate relatives (Lev. 21:1-3)

376. That the sons of Aaron defile themselves for their deceased relatives (by attending their burial), and mourn for them like other Israelites, who are commanded to mourn for their relatives (Lev.21:3)

377. That a Priest who had an immersion during the day (to cleanse him from his uncleanness) shall not serve in the Sanctuary until after sunset (Lev. 21:6)

378. That a Priest shall not marry a divorced woman (Lev. 21:7)

379.That a Priest shall not marry a harlot (Lev. 21:7)

380.That a Priest shall not marry a profaned woman (Lev. 21:7)

381.To show honor to a Priest, and to give him precedence in all things that are holy (Lev. 21:8)

382.That a High Priest shall not defile himself with any dead, even if they are relatives (Lev. 21:11)

383.That a High Priest shall not go (under the same roof) with a dead body (Lev. 21:11)

384.That the High Priest shall marry a virgin (Lev. 21:13)

385.That the High Priest shall not marry a widow (Lev. 21:14)

386.That the High Priest shall not cohabit with a widow, even without marriage, because he profanes her (Lev. 21:15) 387.That a person with a physical blemish shall not serve (in the Sanctuary) (Lev. 21:17)

388.That a Priest with a temporary blemish shall not serve there (Lev. 21:21)

389.That a person with a physical blemish shall not enter the Sanctuary further than the altar (Lev. 21:23)

390.That a Priest who is unclean shall not serve (in the Sanctuary) (Lev. 22:2-3)

391.To send the unclean out of the Camp, that is, out of the Sanctuary (Num. 5:2)

392.That a Priest who is unclean shall not enter the courtyard (Num. 5:2- 3) This refers to the Camp of the Sanctuary 393.That the sons or descendants of Aaron shall bless Israel (Num. 6:23)

394.To set apart a portion of the dough for the Priest (Num.15:20)

395.That the Levites shall not occupy themselves with the service that belongs to the sons of Aaron, nor the sons of Aaron with that belonging to the Levites (Num. 18:3)

396.That one not a descendant of Aaron in the male line shall not serve (in the Sanctuary) (Num. 18:4-7)

397. That the Levite shall serve in the Sanctuary (Num. 18:23)

398. To give the Levites cities to dwell in, these to serve also as cities of refuge (Num. 35:2)

399. That none of the tribe of Levi shall take any portion of territory in the land (of Israel) (Deut. 18:1)

400. That none of the tribe of Levi shall take any share of the spoil (at the conquest of the Promised Land) (Deut. 18:1) 401. That the sons of Aaron shall serve in the Sanctuary in divisions, but on festivals, they all serve together (Deut. 18:6-8)

Tithes, Taxes and T'rumah [Hebrew Offerings]

402. That an uncircumcised person shall not eat of the t'rumah (heave offering), and the same applies to other holy things. This rule is inferred from the law of the Paschal offering, by similarity of phrase (Ex. 12:44-45 and Lev. 22:10) but it is not explicitly set forth in the Torah. Traditionally, it has been learned that the rule that the uncircumcised must not eat holy things is an essential principle of the Torah and not an enactment of the Scribes

403. Not to alter the order of separating the t'rumah and the tithes; the separation be in the order first-fruits at the beginning, then the t'rumah, then the first tithe, and last the second tithe (Ex.22:28)

404. To give half a shekel every year (to the Sanctuary for provision of the public sacrifices) (Ex. 30:13)

405. That a priest [Kohein] who is unclean shall not eat of the t'rumah (Lev.22:3-4)

406. That a person who is not a Kohein or the wife or unmarried daughter of a Kohein shall not eat of the t'rumah (Lev. 22:10)

407. That a sojourner with a Kohein or his hired servant shall not eat of the t'rumah (Lev. 22:10)

408. Not to eat unholy things [Heb. tevel] (something from which the t'rumah and tithe have not yet been separated) (Lev. 22:15)

409. To set apart the tithe of the produce (one tenth of the produce after taking out t'rumah) for the Levites (Lev. 27:30; Num.18:24)

410. To tithe cattle (Lev. 27:32)

411. Not to sell the tithe of the heard (Lev. 27:32-33)

412. That the Levites shall set apart a tenth of the tithes, which they had received from the Israelites, and give it to the Priest [Heb. Kohanim] (called the t'rumah of the tithe) (Num. 18:26)

413. Not to eat the second tithe of cereals outside Jerusalem (Deut.12:17)

414. Not to consume the second tithe of the vintage outside of Jerusalem (Deut. 12:17)

415. Not to consume the second tithe of the oil outside of Jerusalem (Deut. 12:17)

416. Not to forsake the Levites (Deut. 12:19); but their gifts (dues) should be given to them, so that they might rejoice therewith on each and every festival

417. To set apart the second tithe in the first, second, fourth and fifth years of the sabbatical cycle to be eaten by its owner in Jerusalem (Deut. 14:22)

418. To set apart the second tithe in the third and sixth year of the sabbatical cycle for the poor (Deut. 14:28-29)

419. To give the Kohein [i.e. Priest] the due portions of the carcass of cattle (Deut. 18:3)

420. To give the first of the fleece to the priest (Deut. 18:4)

421. To set apart a small portion of the grain, wine and oil for the Priest [Heb. Kohein] [Heb. t'rumah g'dolah i.e. (the great heave-offering) (Deut.18:4)

422. Not to expend the proceeds of the second tithe on anything but food and drink (Deut. 26:14) 423. Not to eat the Second Tithe, even in Jerusalem, in a state of uncleanness, until the tithe had been redeemed (Deut. 26:14)

424. Not to eat the Second Tithe, when mourning (Deut. 26:14)

425. To make the declaration, when bringing the second tithe to the Sanctuary (Deut. 26:13)

The Temple, the Sanctuary and Sacred Objects

426.Not to build an altar of hewn stone (Ex. 20:22)

427.Not to mount the altar by steps (Ex. 20:23) 428.To build the Sanctuary (Ex. 25:8)

429.Not to remove the staves from the Ark (Ex. 25:15)

430.To set the showbread and the frankincense before the Lord every Sabbath (Ex. 25:30)

431.To kindle lights in the Sanctuary (Ex. 27:21)

432.That the breastplate shall not be loosened from the ephod (Ex.28:28)

433.To offer up incense twice daily (Ex. 30:7)

434.Not to offer strange incense nor any sacrifice upon the golden altar (Ex. 30:9)

435.That the Priest shall wash his hands and feet at the time of service (Ex. 30:19)

436.To prepare the oil of anointment and anoint high priests and kings with it (Ex. 30:31)

437.Not to compound oil for lay use after the formula of the anointing oil (Ex. 30:32-33)

438.Not to anoint a stranger with the anointing oil (Ex. 30:32)

439.Not to compound anything after the formula of the incense (Ex.30:37)

440.That he who, in error, makes unlawful use of sacred things, shall make restitution of the value of his trespass and add a fifth (Lev. 5:16)

441.To remove the ashes from the altar (Lev. 6:3)

442.To keep fire always burning on the altar of the burnt-offering (Lev. 6:6)

443.Not to extinguish the fire on the altar (Lev. 6:6)

444.That a Kohein shall not enter the Sanctuary with disheveled hair (Lev. 10:6)

445.That a Kohein shall not enter the Sanctuary with torn garments (Lev. 10:6)

446.That the Kohein shall not leave the Courtyard of the Sanctuary, during service (Lev. 10:7)

447.That an intoxicated person shall not enter the Sanctuary nor give decisions in matters of the Law (Lev. 10:9-11) 448.To revere the Sanctuary (Lev. 19:30) (today, this applies to synagogues)

449.That when the Ark is carried, it should be carried on the shoulder (Num. 7:9)

450.To observe the second Passover (Num. 9:11)

451.To eat the flesh of the Paschal lamb on it, with unleavened bread and bitter herbs (Num. 9:11)

452.Not to leave any flesh of the Paschal lamb brought on the second Passover until the morning (Num. 9:12)

453.Not to break a bone of the Paschal lamb brought on the second Passover (Num. 9:12)

454.To sound the trumpets at the offering of sacrifices and in times of trouble (Num. 10:9-10)

455.To watch over the edifice continually (Num. 18:2)

456.Not to allow the Sanctuary to remain unwatched (Num. 18:5)

457.That an offering shall be brought by one who has in error committed a trespass against sacred things, or robbed, or lain carnally with a bondmaid betrothed to a man or denied what was deposited with him and swore falsely to support his denial. This is called a guilt-offering for a known trespass (Lev. 5:15-19)

458.Not to destroy anything of the Sanctuary, of synagogues, or of houses of study, nor erase the holy names (of God); nor may sacred scriptures be destroyed (Deut. 12:2-4)

Sacrifices and Offerings

459.To sanctify the firstling of clean cattle and offer it up (Ex. 13:2; Deut. 15:19)

460.To slay the Paschal lamb (Ex. 12:6)

461.To eat the flesh of the Paschal sacrifice on the night of the fifteenth of Nissan (Ex. 12:8)

462.Not to eat the flesh of the Paschal lamb raw or sodden (Ex.12:9)

463.Not to leave any portion of the flesh of the Paschal sacrifice until the morning unconsumed (Ex. 12:10)

464.Not to give the flesh of the Paschal lamb to an Israelite who had become an apostate (Ex. 12:43)

465.Not to give flesh of the Paschal lamb to a stranger who lives among you to eat (Ex. 12:45)

466.Not to take any of the flesh of the Paschal lamb from the company's place of assembly (Ex. 12:46)

467.Not to break a bone of the Paschal lamb (Ex. 12:46)

468.That the uncircumcised shall not eat of the flesh of the Paschal lamb (Ex. 12:48)

469.Not to slaughter the Paschal lamb while there is leaven in the home (Ex. 23:18; Ex. 24:25)

470.Not to leave the part of the Paschal lamb that should be burnt on the altar until the morning, when it will no longer be fit to be burnt (Ex. 23:18; Ex. 24:25)

471.Not to go up to the Sanctuary for the festival without bringing an offering (Ex. 23:15)

472.To bring the first fruits to the Sanctuary (Ex. 23:19)

473.That the flesh of a sin-offering and guilt-offering shall be eaten (Ex. 29:33)

474.That one not of the seed of Aaron, shall not eat the flesh of the holy sacrifices (Ex. 29:33)

475.To observe the procedure of the burnt-offering (Lev. 1:3)

476.To observe the procedure of the meal-offering (Lev. 2:1)

477.Not to offer up leaven or honey (Lev. 2:11)

478.That every sacrifice be salted (Lev. 2:13)

479.Not to offer up any offering unsalted (Lev. 2:13)

480.That the Court of Judgment shall offer up a sacrifice if they have erred in a judicial pronouncement (Lev. 4:13) 481.

481.That an individual shall bring a sin-offering if he has sinned in error by committing a transgression (Lev. 4:27-28)

482.To offer a sacrifice of varying value in accordance with one's means (Lev. 5:7)

483.Not to sever completely the head of a fowl brought as a sin-offering (Lev. 5:8)

484.Not to put olive oil in a sin-offering made of flour (Lev. 5:11)

485.Not to put frankincense on a sin-offering made of flour (Lev.5:11)

486.That an individual shall bring an offering if he is in doubt as to whether he has committed a sin for which one has to bring a sin-offering. (Lev.5:17-19)

487.That the remainder of the meal offerings shall be eaten (Lev.6:9)

488.Not to allow the remainder of the meal offerings to become leavened (Lev. 6:10)

489.That the High Priest [Heb. Kohein] shall offer a meal offering daily (Lev. 6:13)

490.Not to eat of the meal offering brought by Aaron and his sons (Lev.6:16)

491.To observe the procedure of the sin-offering (Lev. 6:18)

492.Not to eat of the flesh of sin offerings, the blood of which is brought within the Sanctuary and sprinkled towards the Veil (Lev. 6:23)

493.To observe the procedure of the guilt-offering (Lev. 7:1)

494. To observe the procedure of the peace-offering (Lev. 7:11)

495. To burn meat of the holy sacrifice that has remained over (Lev.7:17)

496. Not to eat of sacrifices that are eaten beyond the appointed time for eating them (Lev. 7:18)

497. Not to eat of holy things that have become unclean (Lev. 7:19)

498. To burn meat of the holy sacrifice that has become unclean (Lev. 7:19)

499. That a person who is unclean shall not eat of things that are holy (Lev. 7:20)

500. A Priest's daughter who profaned herself shall not eat of the holy things, neither of the heave offering nor of the breast, nor of the shoulder of peace offerings (Lev. 10:14, Lev. 22:12)

501. That a woman after childbirth shall bring an offering when she is clean (Lev. 12:6)

502. That the leper shall bring a sacrifice after he is cleansed (Lev.14:10)

503. That a man having an issue shall bring a sacrifice after he is cleansed of his issue (Lev. 15:13-15)

504. That a woman having an issue shall bring a sacrifice after she is cleansed of her issue (Lev. 15:28-30)

505. To observe, on Yom Kippur, the service appointed for that day, regarding the sacrifice, confessions, sending away of the scapegoat, etc. (Lev. 16:3-34)

506. Not to slaughter beasts set apart for sacrifices outside (the Sanctuary) (Lev. 17:3-4)

507. Not to eat flesh of a sacrifice that has been left over (beyond the time appointed for its consumption) (Lev. 19:8) 508. Not to sanctify blemished cattle for sacrifice on the altar (Lev.22:20) This text prohibits such beasts being set apart for sacrifice on the altar

509. That every animal offered up shall be without blemish (Lev.22:21)

510. Not to inflict a blemish on cattle set apart for sacrifice (Lev.22:21)

511.Not to slaughter blemished cattle as sacrifices (Lev. 22:22)

512.Not to burn the limbs of blemished cattle upon the altar (Lev.22:22)

513.Not to sprinkle the blood of blemished cattle upon the altar (Lev. 22:24)

514.Not to offer up a blemished beast that comes from non-Israelites (Lev. 22:25)

515.That sacrifices of cattle can only take place when they are at least eight days old (Lev. 22:27)

516.Not to leave any flesh of the thanksgiving offering until the morning (Lev. 22:30)

517.To offer up the meal-offering of the Omer on the morrow after the first day of Passover, together with one lamb (Lev. 23:10)

518.Not to eat bread made of new grain before the Omer of barley has been offered up on the second day of Passover (Lev.23:14)

519.Not to eat roasted grain of the new produce before that time (Lev. 23:14)

520.Not to eat fresh ears of the new grain before that time (Lev.23:14)

521.To bring on wave loaves of bread together with the sacrifices which are then offered up in connection with the loaves [Pentecost feast] (Lev. 23:17-20)

522.To offer up an additional sacrifice on Passover (Lev. 23:36)

523.That one who vows to the Lord the monetary value of a person shall pay the amount appointed in the Scriptural portion (Lev.27:2-8)

524.If a beast is exchanged for one that had been set apart as an offering, both become sacred (Lev. 27:10)

525.Not to exchange a beast set aside for sacrifice (Lev. 27:10)

526.That one who vows to the Lord the monetary value of an unclean beast shall pay its value (Lev. 27:11-13)

527.That one who vows the value of his house shall pay according to the appraisal of the Priest (Lev. 27:11-13) 528.That one who sanctifies to the Lord a portion of his field shall pay according to the estimation appointed in the Scriptural portion (Lev. 27:16-24)

529.Not to transfer a beast set apart for sacrifice from one class of sacrifices to another (Lev. 27:26)

530.To decide in regard to dedicated property as to which is sacred to the Lord and which belongs to the Priest (Lev. 27:28)

531.Not to sell a field devoted to the Lord (Lev. 27:28)

532.Not to redeem a field devoted to the Lord (Lev. 27:28)

533.To make confession before the Lord of any sin that one has committed, when bringing a sacrifice and at other times (Num.5:6-7)

534.Not to put olive oil in the meal-offering of a woman suspected of adultery (Num. 5:15)

535.Not to put frankincense on it (Num. 5:15)

536.To offer up the regular sacrifices daily (two lambs as burnt offerings) (Num. 28:3)

537.To offer up an additional sacrifice every Sabbath (two lambs) (Num. 28:9)

538.To offer up an additional sacrifice every New Moon (Num. 28:11)

539.To bring an additional offering on the day of the first fruits [Pentecost] (Num. 28:26-27)

540.To offer up an additional sacrifice on [Feast of Trumpets] or Rosh Hashanah (Num.29:1-6)

541.To offer up an additional sacrifice on the day of Atonement or Yom Kippur (Num. 29:7-8)

542.To offer up an additional sacrifice on Feast of Tabernacles [Heb. Sukkot] (Num. 29:12-34)

543.To offer up an additional offering on the eighth day after the feast of Tabernacles called (Heb. Shemini Atzeret), which is a festival by itself (Num. 29:35-38) This eighth day is an anticipation of the New Testament Sabbath which would be instituted on the first day of the week, which is also the eighth day.

544.To bring all offerings, whether obligatory or freewill, on the first festival after these were incurred (Deut. 12:5-6) 545.Not to offer up sacrifices outside (the Sanctuary) (Deut. 12:13)

546.To offer all sacrifices in the Sanctuary (Deut. 12:14)

547.To redeem cattle set apart for sacrifices that contracted disqualifying blemishes, after which they may be eaten by anyone. (Deut. 12:15)

548.Not to eat of the unblemished firstling outside Jerusalem (Deut.12:17)

549.Not to eat the flesh of the burnt-offering (Deut. 12:17). This is a Prohibition applying to every trespasser, not to enjoy any of the holy things.

550.That the sons of Aaron [i.e. his descendants] shall not eat the flesh of the sin-offering or guilt-offering outside the Courtyard (of the Sanctuary) (Deut.12:17)

551.Not to eat of the flesh of the sacrifices that are holy in a minor degree, before the blood has been sprinkled (on the altar), (Deut. 12:17)

552.That the Priest shall not eat the first-fruits before they are set down in the Courtyard (of the Sanctuary) (Deut. 12:17)

553.To take trouble to bring sacrifices to the Sanctuary from places outside the land of Israel (Deut. 12:26)

554.Not to eat the flesh of beasts set apart as sacrifices, that have been rendered unfit to be offered up by deliberately inflicted blemish (Deut. 14:3)

555.Not to do work with cattle set apart for sacrifice (Deut. 15:19)

556.Not to shear beasts set apart for sacrifice (Deut. 15:19)

557.Not to leave any portion of the festival offering brought on the fourteenth of Nissan unto the third day (Deut. 16:4) 558.Not to offer up a beast that has a temporary blemish (Deut.17:1)

559.Not to bring sacrifices out of the hire of a harlot or price of a dog (apparently a euphemism for sodomy) (Deut. 23:19)

560.To read the portion prescribed on bringing the first fruits (Deut.26:5- 10)

Ritual Purity and Impurity

561. That eight species of creeping things defile by contact (Lev.11:29-30)

562. That foods become defiled by contact with unclean things (Lev.11:34)

563. That anyone who touches the carcass of a beast that died of itself shall be unclean (Lev. 11:39)

564. That a lying-in woman is unclean like a menstruating woman (in terms of uncleanness) (Lev. 12:2-5)

565. That a leper is unclean and defiles (Lev. 13:2-46)

566. That the leper shall be universally recognized as such by the prescribed marks So too, all other unclean persons should declare themselves as such (Lev. 13:45)

567. That a leprous garment is unclean and defiles (Lev. 13:47-49)

568. That a leprous house defiles (Lev. 14:34-46)

569. That a man, having a running issue, defiles (Lev. 15:1-15)

570. That the seed of copulation defiles (Lev. 15:16)

571. That purification from all kinds of defilement shall be affected by ceremonial washing (Lev. 15:16)

572. That a menstruating woman is unclean and defiles others (Lev.15:19- 24)

573. That a woman, having a running issue, defiles (Lev. 15:25-27)

574. To carry out the ordinance of the Red Heifer so that its ashes will always be available (Num. 19:9)

575. That a corpse defiles (Num. 19:11-16)

576. That the waters of separation defile one who is clean, and cleanse the unclean from pollution by a dead body (Num.19:19-22)

Lepers and Leprosy

577. Not to drove off the hair of the scall (Lev. 13:33)

578. That the procedure of cleansing leprosy, whether of a man or of a house, takes place with cedar-wood, hyssop, scarlet thread, two birds,

and running water (Lev. 14:1-7)

579.That the leper shall shave all his hair (Lev. 14:9)

580.Not to pluck out the marks of leprosy (Deut. 24:8)

The King

581.Not to curse a ruler, that is, the King in the land of Israel (Ex. 22:27)

582.To appoint a king (Deut. 17:15)

583.Not to appoint as ruler over Israel, one who comes from non-Israelites (Deut. 17:15)

584.That the King shall not acquire an excessive number of horses (Deut. 17:16)

585.That the King shall not take an excessive number of wives (Deut. 17:17)

586.That he shall not accumulate an excessive quantity of gold and silver (Deut. 17:17)

587.That the King shall write a scroll of the Torah for himself, in addition to the one that every person should write, so that he writes two scrolls (Deut. 17:18)

Nazarites

588.That a Nazarite shall not drink wine, or anything mixed with wine which tastes like wine; and even if the wine or the mixture has turned sour, it is prohibited to him (Num. 6:3)

589.That he shall not eat fresh grapes (Num. 6:3)

590.That he shall not eat dried grapes (raisins) (Num. 6:3)

591.That he shall not eat the kernels of the grapes (Num. 6:4)

592.That he shall not eat of the skins of the grapes (Num. 6:4)

593.That the Nazarite shall permit his hair to grow (Num. 6:5)

594.That the Nazarite shall not cut his hair (Num. 6:5)

595.That he shall not enter any covered structure where there is a dead body (Num. 6:6)

596.That a Nazarite shall not defile himself for any dead person (by being in the presence of the corpse) (Num. 6:7) 597.That the Nazarite shall shave his hair when he brings his offerings at the completion of the period of his Nazariteship, or within that period if he has become defiled (Num. 6:9)

Wars

598.That those engaged in warfare shall not fear their enemies nor be panic-stricken by them during battle (Deut. 3:22, 7:21,20:3)

599.To anoint a special Priest (to speak to the soldiers) in a war (Deut. 20:2) This is today's equivalent to a military chaplain.

600.In a permissive war (as distinguished from obligatory ones), to observe the procedure prescribed in the Torah (Deut. 20:10)

601.Not to keep alive any individual of the seven Canaanite nations (Deut. 20:16)

602.To exterminate the seven Canaanite nations from the land of Israel (Deut. 20:17)

603.Not to destroy fruit trees (wantonly or in warfare) (Deut.20:19-20)

604.To deal with a beautiful woman taken captive in war in the manner prescribed in the Torah (Deut. 21:10-14) 605.Not to sell a beautiful woman, (taken captive in war) (Deut.21:14)

606.Not to degrade a beautiful woman (taken captive in war) to the condition of a bondwoman (Deut. 21:14)

607.Not to offer peace to the Ammonites and the Moabites before waging war on them, as should be done to other nations (Deut.23:7)

608.That anyone who is unclean shall not enter the Camp of the Levites (Deut. 23:11)

609.To have a place outside the camp for sanitary purposes (Deut.23:13)

610.To keep that place sanitary (Deut. 23:14-15)

611.Always to remember what Amalek did (Deut. 25:17)

612.That the evil done to us by Amalek shall not be forgotten (Deut.25:19)

613.To destroy the seed of Amalek (Deut. 25:19)

SOURCES AND RESOURCES

The Jews are called the "People of the Book". That is never more apparent until you have written a book on Judaism. I have drawn on, referred to, and been inspired by many texts and websites. This is where I acknowledge those resources.

Arnow, David, Ph.D. *Creating Lively Passover Seders: A Sourcebook of Engaging Tales, Texts & Activities*, Woodstock, VT: JEWISH LIGHTS Publishing, 2004

Charlesworth, James H. *Jesus' Jewishness: Exploring the Place of Jesus in Early Judaism*, New York, NY: The Crossroad Publishing Company, 1991

Erst, Anna Marie, S.H.C.J. *Discovering Our Jewish Roots: A Simple Guide to Judaism*, New York/Mahwah, NJ: Paulist Press, 1996

Evans, Craig A., and Mishkin, David, *A Handbook on the Jewish Roots of the Christian Faith*, Peabody, MA: Hendrickson Publishers, 2019

Fredriksen, Paula. *When Christians Were Jews: The First Generation*, New Haven & London: Yale University Press, 2018

Gillman, Rabbi Neil. *The Jewish Approach to God: A Brief Introduction for Christians*, Woodstock, VT: JEWISH LIGHTS Publishing, 2003

Lotker, Michael. *A Christian's Guide to Judaism*, New York/Mahwah, NJ: Paulist Press, 2004

Morton, Donna Hobeika. *Our Jewish Heritage*, Xulon Press, 2011

Neusner, Jacob. *A Rabbi Talks with Jesus*, Montreal & Kingston: McGill-Queen's University Press, 2000

Robinson, George. *Essential Judaism: A Complete Guide to Beliefs, Customs, and Rituals*, New York, NY: Atria Paperback an Imprint of Simon and Schuster, 2000

Shafiroff, Ira L. *Every Christian's Book on Judaism*, Torrance, CA: Noga Press, 1998

Wilson, Marvin R. *Our Father Abraham: Jewish Roots of the Christian Faith*, Grand Rapids, MI: William B. Erdmans Publishing Company and Dayton, OH: Center for Judaic-Christian Studies, 1989

Zeitlin, Irving M. *Jesus and the Judaism of his Time*, Cambridge, England: Polity   Press, 1988

cojs.org
adDeiGloriam.org
Aish.com
BiblicalArchaeology.org
Chabad.org
CSLewis.org
Hebrew-Streams.org
JewishVoice.org
JewsforJesus.org
MyJewishLearning.com
reasonabletheology.org
religion-online.org
Wikipedia.org